ANTONIO GAUDÍ

antonio gaudí

by George R. Collins

George Braziller, Inc.
NEW YORK

To My Wife

SOURCES OF ILLUSTRATIONS

Album Record a Gaudí (Barcelona, 1936): figure 13

Ampliaciones y Reproduciones MAS, Barcelona: 9, 10, 12, 16, 19, 20, 21, 22, 28, 29, 30, 31, 32, 33, 34, 36, 45, 50, 54, 55, 66, 67, 72, 76, 77, 80, 81, 82, 83, 89, 92, 93, 94, 100, 104, 105, 106, 107; figure 19

Anuario de la Asociación de Arquitectos de Cataluña, 1903: figure 5

Archivo Amigos de Gaudí, Barcelona: 11, 15, 23, 60, 61, 62, 63, 70; figures 8, 18

Archivo Amigos de Gaudí, Barcelona; Foto Aleu: 14, 17, 24, 35, 37, 38, 39, 40, 41, 42, 43, 48, 49, 51, 53, 56, 57, 58, 59, 64, 65, 68, 69, 71, 73, 79, 84, 85, 86, 88, 90, 91, 95, 96, 97, 98, 99, 101, 102; figures 11, 15, 16, 20, 21, 24

Archivo Amigos de Gaudí, Barcelona; Bonet: 46, 47, 75, 78; figure 9

Archivo Amigos de Gaudí, Barcelona; Foto Puig Boada: 74

Archivo Amigos de Gaudí, Barcelona; Foto Casanelles: figures 22, 23

Archivo Histórico de la Cuidad (Barcelona): figure 10

J. Bergós, *Materiales y Elementos de Construcción* (Barcelona, 1953): figure 1

Courtesy of Caja de Ahorros y Monte de Piedad, León: 52

George R. Collins, New York: 1–8, 87*; figures 3, 4**, 6*, 7a*, 7b*, 12

Foto Archivo Brangulí, Barcelona: frontispiece

Foto Imperio, Comillas: 13

El Propagador, 1882: figures 2a, 2b; 1884: figure 14

I. Puig Boada, *El Templo de la Sagrada Familia* (Barcelona, 1952): 18, 25, 26

J. F. Ráfols, *Gaudí* (Barcelona, 1929): 44

J. Rubió, *Tàber Mons Barcinonensis* (Barcelona, 1927): figure 25

A. Zerkowitz, Barcelona: 103

*From originals in possession of Inmobiliaria Provenza, S. A., Barcelona.

**From originals in possession of Amigos de Gaudi, Barcelona.

CONTENTS

Gaudí in the Procession of the Corpus in Barcelona.

AUTHOR'S NOTE

THE CATALAN ARCHITECT Antonio Gaudí has in recent years attracted increasing interest outside of Spain. The purpose of this volume is to make available in English a description of his works and an evaluation of his place in the architecture of his day and of our own. For the specialist there is included what is believed to be a definitive inventory and chronology of his works and a selective bibliography of books and articles on Gaudí and his period. Most of his extant works are illustrated with photographs selected for their architectural qualities. In addition, a number of little-known and recently discovered works by Gaudí will be found among the illustrations.

This book could not have been written without the aid, advice, and hospitality of my friend Enric Casanelles, Secretary of the Amigos de Gaudí of Barcelona. The archive which he is assembling in the Palacio Güell is an indispensable tool for Gaudí studies.

I wish also to express my gratitude to several former associates and friends of Gaudí: Luis Bonet y Garí, Juan B. de Serra Martínez, César Martinell, Juan Matamala Flotats, Isidro Puig Boada, Francisco de Paula Quintana and José F. Ráfols, who have shared so generously with me their recollections and materials pertaining to Gaudí. I have been especially aided by their Excellencies the Bishop of Astorga and the Vizconde de Güell, by the Junta of the Church of the Sagrada Familia, and by the present proprietors and residents of Gaudí's buildings. Father Regulo Casas of the Colonia Güell, Miguel Tubella of the Librería Herederos de la Vda. Pla, José María Guix Sugrañes of Reus and the photographer Francisco Aleu have been particularly helpful. And I am obliged to Señor Bonet and his draughtsmen for allowing me to use their measured drawings, some of which are here published for the first time.

For encouragement and assistance in my researches on the subject I am indebted to Professor Rudolf Wittkower of the Department of Fine Arts and Archaeology, to Mr. Adolph K. Placzek of Avery Architectural Library, and to Miss Mary W. Chamberlin of the Fine Arts Library, all of Columbia University. I would also like to thank Professor James M. Fitch of Columbia University. I have been aided by a grant from the American Council of Learned Societies for the purpose of collecting material on Gaudí, the Gothic Revival, and Modernismo in Spain.

G. R. C.

THE POWER of Antonio Gaudí as an architect lay in his prolific invention of forms. The variety and expressiveness of these forms as sculpture would alone mark him as a notable modern artist. But they were, in fact, the result of unusual structural devices, of an imaginative deployment of materials and of a unique sense of decoration—three traditional attributes of a master builder. Add to these his skill with such intangibles of architecture as space, color and light, and we can understand why the architectural world is today so engrossed in his relatively few and almost forgotten works.

Gaudí, although unique and unheralded as any genius, is not entirely unexplainable. His career coincided with the peak of a movement called the "Renaixença" in Catalonia, that region of Spain where he was born and from which he scarcely stirred throughout his life. During those years Catalonia achieved an economic, political and cultural supremacy which it had not experienced since the period of its independent existence in the later Middle Ages. Commercially and industrially it led Spain and competed with other parts of Europe; it seethed with political movements of all hues, including several varieties of Catalan separatism. The latter groups in particular promoted the revival of their native Catalan tongue and folkways, attaining a truly regional literature and art. The Renaixença in the plastic arts was characterized by phenomenal activity in a variety of styles. In architecture there developed amidst the usual nineteenth-century European eclecticism a serious medieval archaeology and an enthusiastic revivalism of medieval building forms. This was succeeded at the turn of the century by a vigorous outbreak of Art Nouveau, known in its Catalan form as "Modernismo." The earlier movement yielded Gaudí, the later, Picasso.

Regarding patrons to assist him, Gaudí was singularly fortunate. He began his career when Barcelona had burst its old city limits and was expanding feverishly like other European metropolises. The majority of his works were in the new suburbs or in outlying towns that were attaching themselves to the growing city. Furthermore, Gaudí had the luck to attract the attention of a number of wealthy middle-class families and new grandees in Catalonia who catered to his taste for the lavish in architecture, understood and encouraged his most sumptuous projects. His chief Maecenas was Eusebio Güell y Bacigalupi, a textile magnate whose name is almost synonymous with Gaudí's works. (Today his grandson Eusebio Güell y Jover, carrying on the tradition, heads the "Amigos de Gaudí" of Barcelona.)

However, the physical and artistic resources of late nineteenth-century Catalonia might have been lost on Gaudí if it had not been for his peculiar sense of dedication to his craft of building. This consecration was compounded in him by a growing absorption in religion which finally provoked him, in full career, to abandon all secular commissions and to devote himself entirely to the completion of Barcelona's great new church—the Expiatory Temple of the Holy Family—of which he had been architect for nearly 30 years. To Gaudí architecture had an odor of sanctity. For him the architect seemed to be the humble instrument of a Divine Power, and he considered each form he used to be fraught with mystical symbolism.[1] Furthermore, like many of our great contemporary architects, Gaudí seemed to consider his profession to be an apostolic mission—the building of a new Utopia to house and to shape the perfect Society. So we are not surprised to find that, secluded in the workshops of *his* great church in his later life, he would lecture to all visitors, professionals and laymen alike, on any and all aspects of living and building.[2] Oracular utterances they were —he would not abide interruptions—aphorisms not unlike those of his younger contemporary Frank Lloyd Wright.

Although Gaudí was well-read and well-informed about the world outside Spain, that world was, except for occasional tourists and other travellers, rather unaware of him. For more than two decades after his death in 1926 we find him seldom mentioned abroad except in slighting terms. The revived interest in his work today is symptomatic of a crisis in the profession of architecture as our own generation seeks to humanize and to individualize the rather impersonal, cubic and puritanical tradition that we have inherited from our fathers.

LIFE

ANTONI GAUDÍ I CORNET* was born June 25, 1852, in or near Reus in that area of Catalonia known as the Campo de Tarragona (see Chronol., 1852, page 28). As in the rest of Spain, each town and region of Catalonia prides itself on its distinctly individual character or flavor. Much has been made of the fact that Gaudí grew up (1) in Reus which is a bustling little city that has produced a number of important Spanish figures, and (2) amidst the fields of Tarragona which since pre-Roman times have been one of the richest countrysides of the Mediterranean litoral.[3]

Gaudí's origins were humble. His father was a coppersmith, as had been a number of his ancestors.[4] Although one of three children, it would appear that he was denied much of those joys of family life which the Spaniards value so highly and to which his later church of the Sagrada Familia was dedicated. His mother died in his infancy; his brother (a doctor) and his married sister died young. Gaudí himself remained a bachelor,[5] assuming the care of his motherless niece (for whose school in Tarragona he designed chapel furniture in 1880–82) and of his father, both of whom lived with him in Barcelona.

He attended school in Reus, where the secondary institute is now named for him.[6] There his penchant for drawing and for architectural studies was already illustrated in schoolboy projects (see Chronol., 1867–68, 1869–70, page 28). During 1869–70 he went to Barcelona in order to prepare for admission to the new School of Architecture of the University.[7] He did not get his degree until eight years later, having spent considerable time preparing for the school and then in outside architectural work to finance his studies. There also seems to have been a delay for military service between 1874–79. He was an unconventional and somewhat recalcitrant student, perhaps because of his preference for practical work over classroom theory.[8] Gaudí's school accomplishments, academically and artistically, seem

* Throughout this book we have, in most cases, referred to Catalans by the Spanish version of their names, although many of them, like Gaudí, preferred a Catalan spelling such as we use in this instance.

undistinguished and hardly predict the remarkable inventiveness that was to mark his later career.

However, on graduation from architectural school in 1878 he was already well established by virtue of his apprenticeship with a series of important Barcelona builders: Martorell, del Villar and Fontseré. And a showcase which he designed that year for the Paris Exposition brought him to the attention of Eusebio Güell. He attained an almost immediate success as an architect and thenceforth did not leave the environs of Barcelona except for a short trip to southern France, a voyage to Morocco in 1887 and a visit to Castille when he was building the Astorga Palace in 1887–93.

Politically the young man was known as a liberal, although apparently not anti-clerical. It is not clear whether his early project for the workers' cooperative of Mataró was undertaken in sympathy with its political point of view or merely out of financial necessity.[9] He was active in the Catalan movement and eventually became a stalwart of the *Lliga Regionalista,* conservative Catalan party, supporting his friends Francisco Cambó (1876–1947) and Enrique Prat de la Riba (1870–1917), but refusing to stand for office himself.[10] He spoke only in Catalan and with such obstinacy that sometimes his workers had to translate his remarks into Spanish for the benefit of visitors. When on September 11, 1924, the police closed Barcelona's churches to prevent a traditional Catalan celebration, Gaudí protested publicly in the name of the Cult, was jailed and fined. In jail he refused to reply in Castilian Spanish and, characteristically, paid not only his own fine but also that of a poor peddler who had shared his cell.[11]

In this and other matters he was known as an eccentric. For instance, his health. As a child he had incurred a type of rheumatism that never left him. To combat this weakness he adopted the regimen of the Abbott Kneipp[12] which involved, among other things, a frugal vegetarian diet, homeopathic drugs, a variety of bathing procedures and regular hiking—a pattern of behavior that was bound to set him apart. To the end of his life, despite increasing frailty, he continued the long walks.[13] From 1906 he lived in the Park Güell, from which he walked each day to his work at the Sagrada Familia church, a round trip of about four and one-half kilometers. Also each day he attended services at S. Felipe Neri, which was another two kilometers from the Sagrada Familia. Owing to the illness of his usual walking companion and assistant Lorenzo Matamala, he moved from the Park to his studio at the Sagrada Familia church about eight months before his death, but continued to walk to church. It was on such a trip to S. Felipe Neri that he was fatally struck down by a street car.

Equally famous is the apparent dandyism of his youth. Handsome, vain about his appearance and the darling of the artistic and intellectual soirees of the Güell family, Gaudí's early career was certainly in marked contrast to his later anchoritic existence. The sheer lavishness of his great town houses underscores the Franciscan simplicity of those last years when, hat in hand, he went about as a mendicant seeking alms for the works of the Expiatory Temple.[14]

It may have been the growth of his extraordinary religious zeal that brought about this metamorphosis. Finding himself constantly in the service of churches and religious orders (half of his known works and projects were religious in character), he set about systematically to learn more of the church and of its liturgy. For this he relied on books[15] and on contact with a number of learned clerics. Most influential of his religious advisors were Bishop Grau, the compatriot for whom he designed the Episcopal Palace in Astorga; Bishop Campins with whom he planned the liturgical renovation of Palma Cathedral; Father de Valls of the Church of S. Felipe Neri, and the learned Bishop of Vich, Dr. Torras y Bages.[16] Popularly, Gaudí was considered to be something of a saint.[17]

All these traits, combined with his reputation for both wit and irascibility, the common belief that he was a genius, and his life of celibacy—all make him perfect material for a Freudian analysis. Unfortunately the only serious attempt at a psychological study of Gaudí proved to be quite unsuccessful, or at least quite uninteresting.[18]

Most dramatic of all perhaps were the circumstances surrounding Gaudí's death, which were reported in the press of Spain[19] as a civic disgrace and were suffered by Catalans as a national calamity. On the 7th of June, 1926, at about six in the evening, while crossing a busy intersection, Gaudí was hit by a trolley car and severely injured. Unconscious, modestly clad according to his custom, Gaudí was not recognized but was taken for an indigent. Taxis at the scene refused to transport him (for which they were later heavily fined). Finally some passers-by carried him to a local clinic, from which he was transferred, still unidentified, to the Hospital of Santa Cruz in the old quarter of town. It was not for several hours that his absence was noted and friends located him in a pauper's bed of the hospital, on the critical list. They kept a constant vigil, but early on the 10th, without having recovered complete consciousness, he succumbed. From the newspapers of Barcelona, and from elsewhere in Spain, there went up a wail of sorrow and self-incrimination that continued for more than ten days, accounting for a sizeable portion of the vast local literature on Gaudí. On the 12th of June his funeral procession (nearly one-half mile in length) wound from the old hospital to the Cathedral and on to the Sagrada Familia church where he was buried in the crypt by special dispensation of the government and of the Pope. Most of the notables of Catalonia were on hand, and an immense crowd of people lined the four kilometers of streets along the route of the cortege. Special funeral masses were again held on the 17th of June.

It was clear that a great man had died. What legacy had he left?

WORKS

GAUDÍ'S EARLIEST works, including his projects as an architectural student[20] and the commissions in which he collaborated as an apprentice, varied in style between the medieval revival and a rather sumptuous eclecticism that he must have learned in school. Some of them already showed his delight in contrasting materials, such as ironwork against masonry; Barcelona was famous for its wealth of cast-iron decoration, and Gaudí's early designs, especially his street lights, show him to be already expert at this. However, in the big commissions like the medieval *camarín* at Montserrat which he did with the architect del Villar[21] and the Beaux Arts park decorations in Barcelona done with the *maestro* Fontseré,[22] it seems quite impossible to isolate Gaudí's contribution. The Park cascade (plate 9) was, in fact, a frank copy of the Longchamps cascade in Marseilles by Henri Espérandieu, of which they had a photograph.[23]

The two commissions were important ones, as would be a municipal park in the center of modern Barcelona and any work associated with the sacred shrine of Montserrat, but more important for our architect was his association with the medieval revivalist Juan Martorell.[24] Much of Martorell's work seems to be rather ordinary Victorianism to us now, but as a personality he loomed large in the architectural profession of his day. He helped introduce to Catalonia the rational Gothicism of the Frenchman Viollet-le-Duc as well as Ruskin's social interpretation of the style. Martorell was a deeply devout man, much admired by Gaudí, who called him a saint. Gaudí learned greatly from his example and soon succeeded him as the giant of Catalan architecture. His rival in this respect was another young associate of Martorell's, Luis Doménech y Montaner.[25] The enthusiasm for the medieval which architects like Gaudí and Doménech derived from their association with Martorell was further ignited by the influence of Elías Rogent, an originator of the medieval revival in Catalonia and Director of the School of Architecture.[26]

Upon completion of architectural school in 1878, Gaudí lost no time in launching his career. The several works carried out or begun in that year are crucial ones. These include furniture design—an aspect of architecture which he never disdained and which shows him to be in step with the modern desire to weave a complete environment for the patron whenever possible. Invited to design the furniture for Martorell's Gothic chapel in Comillas, he did his medieval best (plates 96–99).[27] This opened to him the patronage of the wealthy family of the Marqués of Comillas, while the interest of Eusebio Güell, who was married to a daughter of the Marqués, was attracted by Gaudí's work for the Exposition of Paris in the same year. Also in 1878 began his association with the workers' cooperative of Mataró.[28] This project was apparently so elaborate, with its machine shed, workers' housing, business and social buildings, that its plans were exhibited at the Paris Exposition. Actually no more than the machinery hall and an adjacent kiosk (fig. 12, page 29) were executed, leaving the architect somewhat disillusioned about such pipe dreams. The shed is a bare, simple building, but of considerable interest structurally (fig. 1). Mechanical efficiency is obtained by the nearly parabolic profile of the arches. Cheapness was achieved by the use of wooden planks throughout, of short length and laminated (three-ply) wherever possible, secured by simple bolts. Today, eighty years later, it is as good as new.

The house that Gaudí started for Manuel Vicens in 1878 was a beginning not only for himself, but also the start of a new tradition in Catalan architecture (plates 10–12). With its novel use of a rich earth-colored rubble bound with brightly-painted tiles (*azulejos*), it marked the complete abandonment of classical and rational design for individual inspiration and whimsy—the final triumph of romanticism over the cold classicism that had characterized Spanish architecture of the early nineteenth century. If Gaudí had recourse to any style of art in the design of the building it was the Moslem. However, Catalonia had had no Moslem tradition, and the Casa Vicens looks like nothing in Spain or in Spanish Africa. Perhaps it should be called "Mudéjar" (the Spanish term for hybrid Moslem)— Gaudí's own mixture of tilework, oddly-shaped arches, *miradors* (look-outs) and lush planting which Spaniards associate with the Moslems. Almost immediately, perhaps influenced by Gaudí, his contemporaries took up the fashion of building in brick or rubble and colored tiles as an economical method. The result was a renaissance of ceramic art all along the eastern litoral of Spain.[29] It is hardly necessary to point out the parallel to this of England's Red House and its Arts and Crafts movement.

As originally built, the Casa Vicens was extremely small, but was decorated inside with a rich eclecticism: ornate Spanish ceilings,

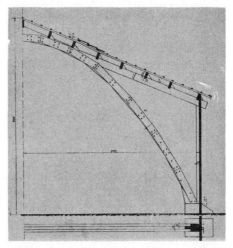

Figure 1. Machine shed in Mataró, 1878–82. Horizontal and vertical sections as drawn by Juan Bergós.

inset panel paintings in the dining room, an oriental *fumador* (smoking room), and a verandah with Japanese blinds. As we see it today, minus its Japanese blinds, it is twice as large and is retracted along the street because of revisions made in 1925–26 by the architect de Serra Martínez under Gaudí's advice (plate 12). De Serra Martínez was able to incorporate Gaudí's unusual cascade arch (now disappeared) into an enlarged garden (plate 10), and he extended Gaudí's iron fence all around the site (plate 11). And de Serra Martínez has interesting things to say about Gaudí's manner of working. It seems that Gaudí built without working drawings on this occasion: the design was controlled by the 15 cm. tile, which he used as a module (Vicens was a tile manufacturer!). Seated in the lot under a parasol (there was a photograph of this), Gaudí indicated directly to the workmen how to proceed. And in that fashion for which he was later to become famous, he frequently made changes, had whole walls ripped out. We are told that Vicens, owner of a modest business, was almost ruined by the expense, but recouped later in the ceramic fad that resulted from the example of this house.[31]

During the 1880s Gaudí designed a number of other buildings of this general "orientalizing" character, although each was distinctly different. The first, a projected hunting pavilion on the coast at Garraf, southwest of Barcelona, was not executed.[32] Then in 1883 he was commissioned to build a house at Comillas as part of the group that Martorell and Doménech were constructing there for the family of the Marqués.[33] Its wandering plan and playful decoration have earned it the title of "El Capricho" (plates 1, 13, 14). Set on a basement of "rusticated" stonework of varying tones, its principal story is built of tan brick banded with strips of gaily-floriated tiles, which parallel the lines of the basement. Then, based on the module of the square flower tile, there rises an intricately corbelled cornice, a series of chimneys and a cylindrical tower, all of which are harmoniously interrelated by patterns such as chevrons and prisms. The suspension of the heavy mass of the tower on top of thin colonettes was to become a favorite (and anti-classical) motif of Gaudí's.

The various works that Gaudí carried out in 1887 for the Güell family on their estate in the suburb of Las Corts in Barcelona might also be classified as orientalizing. Little remains today of this "Finca Güell" except the stables and caretaker's house on a corner of what is now Avenida de la Victoria,[34] between which is the famous dragon gate of ingeniously joined ironwork (plate 39). The plan of the two buildings is an interlocked series of rectangular, square and hexagonal elements. The stable is roofed with a row of small parabolic transverse vaults, constructed of flat Catalan tiles (see page 23), with clerestory lights in the vault ends. In these two edifices the tile courses of Vicens and Comillas have been abandoned, and the soft, almost adobe, brick walls are relieved by stucco surfaces, probably containing cement, into which a simple plate-like mold has been pressed (plate 40). The several cupolas, of which only a small one can be seen in our illustration, are coated with a mosaic of broken tile bits (plate 2). But most subtle is the way in which, to enliven the brick work, Gaudí introduced tiny tile fragments of contrasting colors into the mortar that separates each brick.

His fascination with Moslem art prompted Gaudí in 1887 to make one of his rare excursions out of Catalonia—to Andalusia and Tangier to study it *in situ*. On his return he designed two completely Moorish exposition buildings (1887–88) for the Compañía Trasatlántica—that is to say for the Marqués of Comillas who had taken Gaudí on the trip. Gaudí's interest in Morocco was only natural as Arab themes had been popularized in the painting of such romantics as Mariano Fortuny (of Reus!), and politically Spain was beginning to concern itself with North Africa. The Marqués of Comillas had, in fact, made the Moroccan trip for political reasons, urged by the government to establish Spanish interests there—if possible, a religious mission. Gaudí was taken along to draw up suitable plans for such an institution, which he did for the Marqués in 1892–93 (plate 44).[35] He designed for the use of Franciscan missionaries a vast, several-storied building of circular plan, surrounding a court in which was to rise a large chapel with many steeples. As for its style, it appears that what Gaudí had studied of North Africa was not the lacy Moslem decor, but an indigenous tradition of turreted earthen castles constructed by certain of the Berber tribes. His quest for the Moslem had led him behind it and beyond it to new and unique forms which were to serve him later in other buildings.

Meanwhile Gaudí had been involved in a series of neo-Gothic religious commissions that led up to his appointment as official architect of the Sagrada Familia church. These included chapels and furnishings for schools in San Andrés de Palomar (Barcelona) and in Tarragona, as well as a projected monastery church in the province of Almería. In 1883 Gaudí's former associate del Villar gave up direction of the works of the Sagrada Familia church in a dispute over policy, and Juan Martorell, who had precipitated the situation, recommended Gaudí as his successor. The circumstances that had brought about construction of this Expiatory Church of the Holy Family are of importance to us. It should be understood that it was dedicated to: (1) the Holy Family as the exemplar of the virtues of domestic life, (2) Saint Joseph as patron of the working class, and (3) the expiation of the sins of a materialistic age. It was to be financed entirely by alms, viz., by donations rather than by the regular income of the Church or State. This all came about through the efforts of a pious gentleman of Barcelona, José María Bocabella y Verdaguer (1815–92) and his priest, the Mercedarian José María Rodriguez (1817–79). Impressed by a French Marist publication dedicated to the cult of St. Joseph,[36] Bocabella founded in Barcelona in 1866 the Asociación de Devotos de San José and began publication of a version of the French magazine entitled *El Propagador de la Devoción de San José*. Together with Father Rodriguez, he achieved phenomenal success, raising a large donation for the Vatican by 1872. In 1874–75 they conceived the idea of their own church, to be a copy of the famous shrine at Loreto in Italy with a replica of the miraculous house of Nazareth in its crypt. For this in 1881 they bought a large site in the suburb of Gracia, engaging del Villar, who was diocesan architect, in 1882. He convinced them to change to a neo-Gothic style, and ground was broken for the church on the feast day of St. Joseph in 1882. Del Villar's original plans were very conventional (figs. 2a and b),[37] but under Gaudí's management the neo-Gothic was gradually converted to an entirely unique style, and the building itself became, at times, an almost international symbol of religious quixotism (plate 19).

The significance of this edifice to nineteenth-century Barcelona, beset as it was with labor unrest and anti-clericalism, was immense, and the project seems to have become a rallying point for the religious political parties and for such conservative or centrist newspapers as *El Correo Catalán, Diario de Barcelona, La Publicitat, La Vanguardia* and *La Veu de Catalunya,* which for years reported its progress almost daily.[38] Both Bocabella and Gaudí expressed the desire that the church become the center of a colony of schools and that craftsmen's shops be clustered about it[39]—a romantic reconstruction of the devout Middle Ages. But apart from its moral and doctrinal implications, the building quickly became the symbol of the expansion of Barcelona as a city, of the modern metropolis over against the old medieval center. Juan Maragall voiced this when in 1905 he exclaimed, "The city shows proudly to all strangers its temple a-building; the temple ennobles the material expansion of the city; soon Barcelona will be the city of *that* temple, and it appears that the temple cannot exist but for *that*

Figure 2a, b. Two engravings of del Villar's first project for the Sagrada Familia church as published in *El Propagador,* official organ of the enterprise, in 1882.

city; they are forever united." [40] When its towers were completed in the 1920s it became, in fact, Barcelona's skyscraper and figured so in many picture books. *The New York Times Magazine* and *The Illustrated London News* selected it as characteristic of the New Barcelona. [41]

A good idea of Gaudí's early ecclesiastical style can be obtained from the newly-discovered project for an altar in the town of Alella near Barcelona, dated July 1883 just before he took over the Sagrada Familia works (plate 15). Intricately neo-Gothic, it relies heavily on the effect of an inscription repeated endlessly. Such calligraphy was frequently to be a basis of his architectural ornament. Gaudí's original project for the exterior of the Sagrada Familia was very neo-Gothic, differing from del Villar's second plans only in being more complex and pointed (fig. 13, page 30). However, as we can see from his later designs (plate 22) Gaudí was to leave the Gothic Revival far behind, apparently under the influence of his own Tangier studies (plate 44). In completing the crypt, of which del Villar had left a beginning, Gaudí heightened the vaults so that it would have more light and air. He may already have sensed that the crypt would long be the only covered place for religious worship—as it remains today. Certainly he never dreamed that he would finish the whole church. "Such a work," he said, "must be the product of a long period; the longer the better . . . The work of a single man remains necessarily meager and dies when scarcely born." [42] Again he remarked, "It will be the master Saint Joseph who finishes it . . ." [43] The completion of the crypt and the raising of the chevet walls and pinnacles took him until about 1893. Being a fairly straightforward Gothic revivalism this interests us little except to note that the foliated pinnacles derive from his favorite authority, Viollet-le-Duc, as do the flowering crosses that terminate many of his secular buildings. [44]

Progress on the church was, of course, hampered by the quantity of other projects in which Gaudí was concerned during the late 1880s and the 1890s. Foremost among these

14

was the town house which he constructed for Eusebio Güell (plate 28). The Palacio Güell, as it is called, is remarkable for the quantity of activities that the architect worked into a small site, for its highly original forms, and for the extremely modern sense of flowing space. A glance at the section (plate 27) will show that the great parabolic entrance arches (plate 30) lead into a vestibule in which guests were to dismount from horses and vehicles (plate 33). Carriages were parked in the large hall behind the stairs, horses led down the spiral ramp (plate 38) to the cellar stables. Guests arrived at the main rooms (*piano nobile*) by a series of monumental stairways (plate 33). Here there is a large central room (with organ and side chapel) going up through several floors (plate 27)—a grand, galleried space for which he may have been inspired by the huge open stair hall of Martorell's palace at Comillas (see note 24). Arcading, windows and wooden fretwork are used to divide the sumptuous side rooms from this hall and from each other in such a way that they do not distinctly separate (plate 34). There was a terrace garden outside as well as a number of running balconies and arcades inside that heighten this effect of continuous space. Even ceiling surfaces were made imprecise by intricate craftsmanship (plate 35), and inert stone was brought to life by applying to it a sort of proto-Art Nouveau ironwork (plate 36). As for the lighting, ingenious blinds were devised for the main rooms (plate 31), and the hall cupola was perforated with tiny windows that gave the impression of stars, by day from the natural light and at night from inset light bulbs—a modern trick. The outer shell of this cupola was the major element among the chimney pots and ventilator tops of his roof terrace (plate 32). Fortunately heating in Catalonia is not central but 'anarchic,' and Gaudí was always provided with the constituents for constructing a whimsical landscape of chimneys among the clothes-lines of Spanish rooftops. Here as at the Finca Güell he employed his mosaics of broken tile bits. Among modernities too numerous to mention are the parabolic arches (plate 30), the mushroom columns and helical shapes (plates 37, 38). As American magazines observed in 1892, cost was no factor with Güell and Gaudí.[45] It seems inevitable that the owner of this palace should have later been made a count! [46]

This building, which was perhaps Venetian Gothic in origin and which Gaudí himself called "meager Viollet-le-Duc,"[47] was the first of a series of his residences that might be taken together as Gothic Revival. Of these the Episcopal Palace in Astorga (near León) of 1887–93 was equally ambitious; but it is difficult to reconstruct Gaudí's intentions from that which remains today (plates 41–43). In 1886 Gaudí was asked to build the palace by the new Bishop Grau, who was from Reus and knew the works of the Sagrada Familia. As he could not leave his work on the Palacio Güell at that time, Gaudí carried on a long correspondence with the Bishop about the customs and countryside of León and immersed himself in books about that province in order to produce a building true to the region. In August 1887 he sent on the plans. They delighted the Bishop, but were held up for two years by those officials in Madrid who controlled ecclesiastical and public works. Gaudí went on himself in 1889 to supervise the construction, which was carried out by imported Catalan artisans. When the bishop died in 1893 the work was taken out of Gaudí's hands and entrusted to local builders who did not understand his vaulting—with resultant collapses and other disastrous consequences. The present building (plate 41) conforms in very few respects to the plans Gaudi signed (fig. 3). Gaudí was a great improviser, and the plans he was required to present to officials or patrons seldom revealed his final intentions. In this case he is said to have found Astorga so different from what he had imagined that he spent a long time after his arrival recasting the project. For instance, the lower portions and in particular the porch (plate 42) became much more powerful than in the original plans. The fact is that he grew tremendously in stature during this ill-fated commission. It

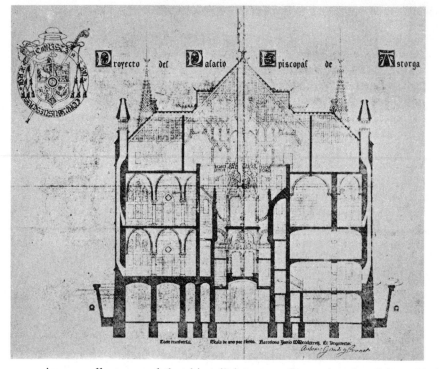

Figure 3. Section of the Palacio Episcopal of Astorga as planned (and signed) by Gaudí in 1887.

is generally assumed that his religious transformation dated from his long discussions with Bishop Grau on the subjects of episcopal dignity, the hierarchy, the liturgy and architecture.[48]

While Gaudí was in the region he was invited by some textile merchants who knew the Güells to construct a building for them on the old Plaza de San Marcelo in the city of León. In keeping with the venerable traditions of the city and the great bulk of the Casa de los Guzmanes (1560) nearby, Gaudí erected his plainest, sternest building which, for once, was carried out exactly as he drew it (plate 52). Called the Casa Fernández-Andrés (for the owners) or "Casa de los Botines" for a former proprietor of their firm, it is probably his most businesslike structure as well. It is a compact, rock-faced cube. Its ground floor and basement were devoted to the business, and the upper floors contained apartments of simple quadrilateral rooms grouped about six narrow light-courts (fig. 4). His usual lavishness occurs only at the main door (plate 51) and in ceilings of the proprietors' apartment (plate 53).[49]

In Barcelona, meanwhile, Gaudí had been occupied with another large building, the convent school of Santa Teresa de Jesús (1889–94). This was another instance of the association of Gaudí with the Catalan religious revival; the order of the Compañía de Santa Teresa was a new one, having been founded there in 1876. Externally their building (plate 45) is also a simple block, relieved by the presence of a crowning cornice, large flowered crosses at the corners and an entrance pavilion which is similar to that of the Tangier mission (plate 44). The interior (plates 49, 50) is sparse, each brick exploited structurally to the full in order to achieve the greatest economy of materials. As can be seen from our diagrams and photographs (plates 46–50), the interior is built up of superimposed arcades of a steep parabolic profile that is achieved by projecting the bricks horizontally (corbelling) up to the crest where there is a short arch of radially arranged bricks. This unit is bulky but light, and it appears to have no sidewise thrusts. Its tall shape was made the motif of the external wall design, giving the whole a vaguely Moorish flavor which, with his use of brick and rubble, unites it with the houses we discussed earlier (pages 11–13).

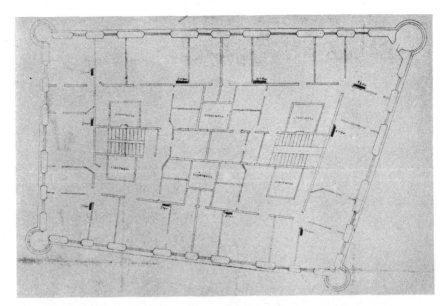

Figure 4. Plan of the proprietors' floor of the Casa Fernández-Andrés in León. The upper floors are similar, but are divided into four apartments instead of two.

Any effort to divide Gaudí's highly individualized buildings into "style" groups is self-defeating because historical styles were exactly what he was growing away from in his search for personal expression. However, up to about 1900 the imprint of tradition is clear in his buildings in contrast to his output after that date. The last of what we might call his neo-Gothic designs is "Bell Esguard," a villa built in 1900–02 for the widow of Jaime Figueras high above the city on the remains of a palace that had belonged to a monarch of Catalonia's Gothic age (plate 64). The medieval aspect of this building was now an archaism for Gaudí, retained undoubtedly out of respect for the tradition of the site.[50] The tall castellated shape of the house would be attributable to the same romanticism. (Incidentally, the Catalan word for a country villa is *torre,* literally "tower.") Not appreciable in photographs is the fact that the roof top is a maze of stairways, galleries and lookouts from which a vast panorama of Barcelona and its port can be seen spread out below. Under the high roof is the first of Gaudí's fabulous garrets (*desvanes*) (plate 65). Oddly contrived vaults also appear downstairs under a plaster coating. But the most appealing feature of "Bell Esguard" is the low-keyed chromatic character of its rubble walls, produced by selecting brownish, yellowish and greenish stone of the area (plate 4). With this building religious symbolism begins to dominate his secular commissions. Not only is there a large floral cross (again adapted from Viollet-le-Duc), but in the window over the door is a green star that was to have been part of a scene of the Three Magi, and in the ironwork of the door is written, "María Purissima: sens pecat fou concebuda."

About 1900 Gaudí became involved in a project of urbanism. Eusebio Güell had purchased a large property on the slopes of a bare mountain behind Barcelona. Here he had the intention of creating a village development on the model of English gardens.[51] Gaudí worked on this "Park Güell," as it was called, from 1900–14, covering the hillsides (plate 66) with a series of serpentine galleries and viaducts that followed closely the irregularities of the terrain (fig. 5). Some sixty carefully-regulated building sites of triangular format were provided, but only three houses were ever built. After the death of Don Eusebio the property passed to the city, which now maintains it as a very successful public park.

The main elements of the Park: The principal entrance with its two bizarre gate houses

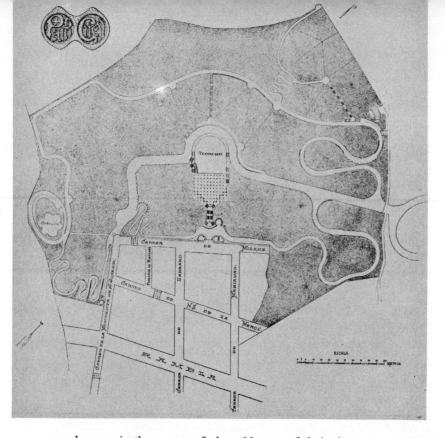

Figure 5. Original plan of the Park Güell of Barcelona, before revisions were made.

can be seen in the center of plate 66; two of their three turrets rise above their warped tile roofs in plate 68. The entrance stairway leads past two dripping fountains (representing a snake and a giant lizard) to the "market" hall, whose vaulted roof is supported on 100 large archaic Doric columns, the outside ones leaning inward to meet the transverse thrusts of the load (plate 67). Above and in part carried by the market columns is a large open Greek theater, the level "orchestra" of which is bounded by a serpentine ceramic bench and now serves as a playground (plates 3, 69). Through the rest of the park more or less as in his original plan (fig. 5) Gaudí laid out several kilometers of viaduct, carried for much of its length upon inclined piers of rough stone that make up galleries (plates 70, 71), sometimes of two superimposed levels. At the highest point, which provides a breath-taking view of the Mediterranean, was planned at first a chapel and then a giant cross, the usual dominating accent for Gaudí's works.[52]

Gaudí's intention was to be bizarre and playful on the one hand, and on the other to produce an architecture that was a complement to Nature, rather than a contrast to it. That he was successful in his first purpose is testified to by the delight that the Surrealists have always taken in this Park. Salvador Dalí recollects, "The open spaces between the artificial trees gave me a sensation of unforgettable anguish."[53] As to his second purpose, Gaudí had by now sloughed off the last vestiges of historicism in his architecture (a struggle that was not generally resolved elsewhere in Europe until considerably later). He still could play with the Doric Order in the Park and archaeologically restore the Gothic cathedral on Mallorca. However, in his serious creative moments he now had recourse to Nature. His idea was not to reconstruct natural forms exactly nor simply to stylize them anew as much Art Nouveau was doing, but to produce a type of poetic metamorphosis of

18

them, working according to natural laws, which he considered to be the primary rules of the art of architecture.[54] Thus, without breaking with the innate properties of building materials, one could create forms parallel to, or evocative of, the beauties of Nature (that is to say, of God's architecture, which as Gaudí observed has no straight lines in it). The resultant architectural forms are not to be found in Nature, and yet they speak to us directly of it, without using intermediary literary symbols. It would seem to be such a creative process as this that causes his later works to evoke clear but indefinable natural sensations and brings Gaudí into line with much twentieth-century painting and sculpture. It is conceivable that Gaudí was influenced by the writings of Goethe on architecture and on Nature; this poet was exerting a profound effect on Catalan intellectuals, and his works were in Gaudí's library.[55] Or such a conception of architecture as a metamorphosis of Nature's forms could have been suggested by Ruskin's inspired passages about Nature and the Gothic,[56] and so have been derived directly from Gaudí's medieval interests.

Of course, one of the most startlingly "live" aspects of Gaudí's late buildings is his use of inclined supports. These he employed in order to avoid buttresses, which he called "crutches," and to put all the strength of his piers directly into the line of support. Regarding concrete, although the Güell industries manufactured a fine quality cement, Gaudí used it for little except stuccoing, as on the upper surface of the Doric columns of the Park. These columns were made of structural tiles and were left hollow in the center to conduct into a large irrigation cistern the water that filtered through the porous soil of the playground. Supported here on the columns *is* a framework of reinforced concrete beams (apparently the only ones Gaudí ever used), on which were set the flat tile domes that actually carry the soil above. It is on the under surface of these domes that the famous "collages" of shattered tiles, bottles, cups, saucers, etc., were composed by Gaudí's assistant Jujol.[57]

Modernismo,[58] the Spanish Art Nouveau, developed within the Catalan Renaixença over the turn of the century. It was stimulated by the Art Nouveau of Paris, where many Catalan intellectuals resided, and by the similar Jugendstil movement of Germany. Gaudí had already employed some of the most characteristic Art Nouveau elements, such as long curvilinear forms and freely-stylized plants, in his buildings as early as the mid 1880s—well in advance of Art Nouveau elsewhere. We have noticed this in the Palacio Güell (plates 29, 36), and it is particularly vivid in his furniture of this epoch (plates 100–102).

The Casa Calvet (1898–1904) is the building by Gaudí that best typifies the nascent Modernismo.[59] The facade (plate 54) is a rather conventional Barcelona one, enlivened here and there by the fluid rococo and Art Nouveau details that appeared together at this moment. The latter are most advanced in the iron derricks at the top, in the plant motifs of the owner's oriel window and in tiny fronds amongst the iron balconies. Inside one can see from the luxuriant decoration of the elevator stairwell (plate 55) that something is stirring and that it is related to vegetation and flowing stone. Throughout this stairwell a fresh growth of nature is evident, although not as stringy as in most Art Nouveau; except for the door handles, which look like van de Velde's or Guimard's, the Casa Calvet's Modernismo is an independent local variety.[60] Gaudí seems closest to European Art Nouveau in the furniture he designed for the ground floor offices (plates 105–107). On the whole, however, this building seems to be the most conservative of all his works, as testified to by its receiving a prize from the municipality. It was the municipality's first such building prize and Gaudí's only one; his lesser contemporaries (Doménech y Montaner, Puig y Cadafalch, Sagnier[61]) were to win several each. In its day the Casa Calvet was considered Churrigueresque (Spanish late Baroque).[62]

However, guided by his pursuit of Nature and its forms, Gaudí went directly into a more robust, structural and three-dimensional style than is characteristic of the Art Nouveau in Spain and elsewhere in Europe. His buildings can usually be distinguished at a glance from those of even his closest followers.[63] This may also have resulted because, chronologically, he developed this phase while he was planning the transept and portals of the Sagrada Familia church (1891-1903), so that his Art Nouveau is a direct outgrowth of the Gothic and the structural. The transept facade (plates 16, 17), except for some later figure sculpture, was carried out after his return from Astorga and seems to be, with its dripping stone effects, his first large Modernista work. His design for a sanctuary at Reus in 1900 (fig. 16, page 31) is almost too sketchy to judge, but seems to be in keeping with the Sagrada Familia portal. Then, chronologically, would come the furniture for the Casa Calvet offices of about 1901 (plates 105-107) and the entrance houses of the Park Güell (plate 68) which were finished before 1903. The Graner chalet of 1904 (Chronol., 1904, page 31) was to have been a larger version of the Park gate houses, but a bit less spiralized and more spacious. Thus the warped surfaces which are characteristic of Gaudí's mature work appear to have been developed by him between 1900 and 1902 in the roofs of the Park houses and in the enclosure for the Miralles estate of 1901-02 (plates 72, 73). In the masonry of the latter no straight line is to be found.[64] This work at the Park and at the *finca* Miralles prepares us then for the complete three-dimensionality of his last two secular buildings—the Casa Batlló and the Casa Milá.

The Casa Batlló (1905-07) is a good example of Gaudí's image of architecture as deified Nature (plate 76). The iridescent tiles of the facade recall the bubbly surface of a Mediterranean wave spreading over a rocky beach. The kelp-like metal work of the upper balconies and the weedy-green coping (plate 8) enhance this effect. But the balconies also appear to be masks and relate somehow to the organic skeletal aspect of the lower facade (plate 77). Meanwhile a succession of tiles inch their way along the crowning molding, changing color as they go (plate 8), and the ever-present cross grows like some strange flower, well above it all. The vestibule and central court (plates 75, 79) are tiled in white and light blues, contributing further to the general marine effect. However, in marked contrast, attic and skylight (plates 80, 81) are very mechanical if still somewhat eerie. Of the entry (plate 82) and dining room (plate 83) of the principal level, one need remark only that the architect has avoided straight lines at all costs. This is also observable in the floor plan (plate 78) which is a work of art in itself. The rooms were scattered about with his chairs, offering themselves for the comfort of weary bodies. The form of the small chair is so appealingly sculptural that it has been presented in recent exhibitions on a pedestal, as though it were a piece of modern art.

We have come a long way since the Casa Calvet of less than a decade earlier (compare plates 54 and 76). Everything has loosened up, and the facade of Batlló is such an enveloping affair that it is scarcely apparent that Gaudí here has merely remodelled a front that was like Calvet's and which still retains rectangular openings for the majority of its windows. We might also compare Batlló with the adjoining facade to its left in plate 76, which was designed in 1900 by Puig y Cadafalch, one of Gaudí's outstanding competitors.[65] Although designed by one of the most lavish and imaginative of his Renaixença rivals, it remains flat, static, symmetrical and, of course, historically derivative, by comparison with the Casa Batlló.[66]

In contrast to the shimmering aqueous qualities of the Casa Batlló, the nearby Casa Milá (1905-10) on the Paseo de Gracia seems to be a man-made mountain (plate 86). Popularly known as "la Pedrera" (the quarry), its color is somber, its stone hammered and pitted.[67] It, too, has something to do with Nature: it has been likened to rocks of the Pyrenees,[68] to human lips and (in caricatures) to pastries and hornets' nests. It, too, is Mediterranean, as can be surmised from its sea-weed balconies, the grotto-like entrance courts (plate 92) and interior ceilings which resemble the patterns left in the sand by a wave (plate 93).[69] Nor is it solid rock. Gaudí, no purist, used materials to suit his purpose. Many of the jutting stones are supported by interior ironwork; some balconies are not stone at all, but are made of metal beams with glass flooring in order to allow light through to the apartment below (plate 88). And many horizontal metal beams are necessary to support the numerous piers and wall sections that stand above windows (plate 86). The pattern of these windows and supports is maddeningly random—like designs by Paul Klee —and wilfully anti-classical.

The pride of this building is its roof, a lunar landscape of erratic up and down stairways as in a dream (plate 89). It is inhabited by bizarre ventilators and chimneys, which at first seem to be sheer whimsy (plates 90–91). But when it is realized that the whole building was to be the base for a gigantic statue of the Virgin de la [Paseo de la] Gracia, the demonic versus chivalric appearance of these figures is understandable. The cornice had been prepared in honor of the Virgin with the inscription, "Ave . . . gratia . . . plena . . . Dominus . . . tecum" (plate 86). When, after the destruction of religious buildings that accompanied the uprising in Barcelona in 1909, the proprietor begged off for fear that her building would be taken for a convent, Gaudí lost interest in the whole project and left it to assistants to finish. The rise and fall of the terraces of this roof is a result of the varying height of the parabolic arches of the garret (plate 94, fig. 6), which in turn arises from the fact that the garret arches must span floors of varying breadth.

Although the structure is basically a simple one (fig. 6), each floor plan is remarkably complex and different from the next. Illustrated here are two of Gaudí's original floor plans, which do not correspond at all to actuality (figs. 7a, 7b), because the present parti-

Figure 6. Gaudí's original sectional drawing of the Casa Milá.

21

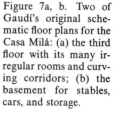

Figure 7a, b. Two of Gaudí's original schematic floor plans for the Casa Milá: (a) the third floor with its many irregular rooms and curving corridors; (b) the basement for stables, cars, and storage.

tions were installed after the building was constructed. This was done so as to ensure the maximum light and the most flowing sense of space possible. The plaster decoration of ceilings and moldings varies radically from room to room and appears to have been modeled on the spur of the moment, sometimes with the hands or fingers (plate 93). It is also interesting to note that Gaudí sold the Milás a building very much like the Casa Batlló (plate 87), but changed his plan extensively before construction started.

The Casa Batlló and the Casa Milá demonstrate that Gaudí was pursuing something more universal in Nature than the floral ornament and whiplash lines of his Modernista compatriots. Typical Art Nouveau we tend to find only in the detailing (plate 104) and in the decorations that he left to such assistants as Jujol. Gaudí had himself become increasingly absorbed in the mechanics of architecture and in its underlying geometry. He was particularly interested in the structural properties of what are called "ruled surfaces," regularly warped shapes such as hyperbolic paraboloids, that are probably most familiar to us in the sculptures

22

of Gabo and Pevsner of the 1930s. These studies he was pursuing in connection with two religious projects, the Sagrada Familia church and the Colonia Güell chapel, in favor of which in 1910 he withdrew from almost all his other work. His reasons for the latter action need still to be explored psychologically. Taste in Catalonia was veering away from him in a typical classicistic reaction against Modernismo.[70] The big exposition of his works in Paris in 1910 (see Chronol., 1910, page 32) had received favorable comment, but it was clear that the world was not ready for Gaudí's architecture.[71] Gaudí himself insisted about his abandonment of all but his religious commissions, "I have no family, nor obligations; I have left my clients, I have refused commissions; I do not wish to work for other than the Sagrada Familia, I wish nothing but it . . . what I am doing is my duty, nothing more, and I must do it." [72] He did, however, continue with his work at the Cathedral of Mallorca until 1914. This was, after all, an effort to adapt the cathedral to modern liturgy and was therefore closely related to the liturgical planning of the Sagrada Familia church (plates 25, 26).[73]

In his search for economy and efficiency in his structures, Gaudí relied on the ancient Catalan technique of tile vaulting in which the tiles are laid edge to edge and the vaults are strengthened by stiffener ribs or diaphragm arches (plate 94).[74] He carried out studies of the weights of available building stones in order to find a light, strong material for his masonry vaults.[75] What he was aiming at can be seen in the school building (plate 95) which he erected in 1909 beside the church of the Sagrada Familia using the *bóvedas tabicadas* (board vaults) resting on beams. Here the undulating vault surface can, as seen in figure 8, be calculated and built with ease, and a similar undulation of the vertical walls stiffens them as well. Such shapes are the last word today in egg-shell concrete structures.[76] And then there were the inclined piers which we have already discussed in connection with the Park Güell (page 19). Combined with his parabolic arches, the inclined pier brought most of his supporting masonry under compression, thus increasing its efficiency. The final step was to vault his buildings with hyperbolic paraboloid surfaces as in the latest model for the Sagrada Familia church (plate 24). Such geometrical surfaces are of great mechanical efficiency and, despite their complex appearance and long name, they can be described simply by means of straight lines and erected on forms composed of straight planks. Gaudí considered this to be a miracle of mathematics and, as we have seen (note 1), attributed holy properties to the *Trinity* of straight lines which determine any such surface.

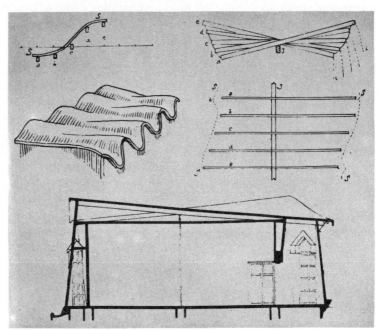

Figure 8. Diagrams and a transverse section illustrating how the helicoidal form of the roof of the Sagrada Familia schools was obtained by laying the tile surface on wooden cross beams (a, b, c . . .) which teeter asymetrically upon a central metal beam J as their ends follow the helix S–S. Projecting lips at the low points of the roof throw water free of the walls which, being perpendicular to the beams (a, b, c . . .), are also helicoidal.

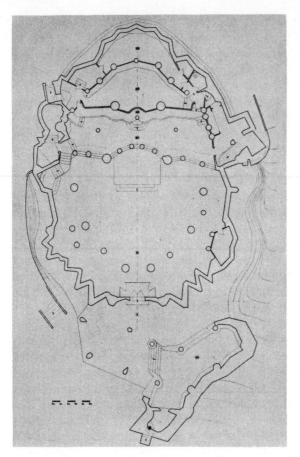

Figure 9. Ground plan of the workers' chapel at the Colonia Güell near Barcelona, 1898–1915, as drawn for the architect Luis Bonet y Garí.

The real laboratory for all these structural and geometrical speculations was the chapel at the Colonia Güell, a workers' settlement for the Güells' textile factories outside of Barcelona. Gaudí was presented with the commission in 1898, but did no more than the theoretical calculations during the first ten years. Construction began in 1908, proceeded slowly; only the crypt of the chapel was ever finished (plate 56, fig. 9). His sketches for the finished structure can be seen in plates 60, 61. A glance at the crypt (plates 5, 56–59) will explain why the calculations evolved so slowly and the work took so long. The form and the textures are incredibly complicated in relationship to each other. To appreciate this, follow any support or shape through its several transformations—Nature and architecture are here in metamorphosis! Materials include tile fragments, rough basalt, bricks; and the grilles are forged out of scrap iron.

Mechanically the most fascinating thing about the Colonia Güell construction is the model that Gaudí devised for his workers to follow (plates 62–63). This was a scale model of a funicular diagram of the stresses. A number of funiculars (non-elastic cords suspended from both ends) were hung equal to the number of arches and ribs of the proposed building (plate 63). At appropriate points weights were hung on the funiculars corresponding to the load that the arch or rib would be required to carry at that point. The funicular curve is thus distorted into a polygonal form whose sides show the inclinations that are necessary in the arches, ribs, and piers in order for them to meet the thrusts of the loads in question. When the photograph is inverted (as we print it here), one sees a structure roughly conforming to the interior (plate 61). By suspending weights from sheets instead of from cords, the properly warped *surfaces* were obtained (plate 62). Exacting calculation of the weights was necessary, but the complex vaults could be erected without extensive preparatory drawings. The system has application to modern concrete construction.[77] This crypt, although only a fragment of a building, is perhaps the most interesting of Gaudí's works for us today.[78]

On the other hand, the Sagrada Familia church suffers because its most exciting portions have never been carried out. Following the completion of the portal gables (about 1903) work on the towers proceeded very slowly, the masonry of the first one not being completed until 1918. The openings in these towers are shuttered for acoustical purposes; they are to have long cylindrical bells, one of which was successfully tried out in 1915. The cubistic pinnacles took about another decade to finish (plate 7), the last of the glass mosaic being applied in 1930. The interlocking geometric forms of these pinnacles are fascinating to analyze (plate 18). Conical holes were pierced through at two-thirds the height of the pinnacles in order to accomodate spot lights, to be directed down to the street in front, and in back to light up the great ciborium that was planned for the crossing. Besides acoustics and illumination, Gaudí was also concerned with color—the portals were to be painted, each in a different hue to symbolize its meaning: Faith-yellow, Hope-green, and blue for Charity. The iconography of the whole project is a study in itself—a fascinating *Summa Theologica* of the modern Church and the culmination of many years of research by Gaudí and his religious advisers (plates 25–26).[79] Of the many parts which he sketched for the building, we illustrate only Gaudí's drawing for the other transept, that of the Passion designed about 1917 (plate 20).[80] Like this portal, the projected nave (plates 23–24) shows many consequences of the Colonia Güell experiments—for instance, the prismatic treatment of the upper piers. The relation of these branching piers to the hyperbolic paraboloid vaults is that each carries its own vault section like an umbrella, so that the structure will approximate a series of columns with their capitals. Gaudí, before his death, toyed with the idea of vaulting the building with concrete; as can be seen from plate 23 there are to be many structural complications above the vaults themselves. He had moved far from the mechanical revival of Gothic masonry techniques which he learned in his youth. When asked as early as 1908 by a visitor, "Is this the last of the cathedrals?" Gaudí replied, "No, it is the first of a new series."[81]

Gaudí did not leave us an explicit architectural theory. He apparently never delivered a lecture nor wrote an article or book. What we have instead is a collection of dictums handed on to us by his associates, by visitors or by the press. These have been collected and published like the sayings of an oriental holy man, a great deal of literature having been devoted to their exegesis.[82] Some of his remarks are so cryptic as to have been explained variously: "Originalidad es volver al origen," has been taken to mean to return to fundamentals, to go primitive, form following function, or the return to God. Others are more complete. As an example, he spoke often of light, being concerned particularly with the angle of inclination of natural light and insisting, "Architecture is then Mediterranean, because it is harmony of light and this does not exist in the countries of the North which have an unhappy horizontal light, nor in the tropical countries where the light is vertical." He talked much of Mediterraneanism, even attributing to it the Gothic style. His great masters were the Greeks, for whom he expressed a most uncritical enthusiasm, while always belittling the Gothic as an incompletely evolved and an "industrial" architecture. He had a rather mystical belief in environment and family tradition. He ascribed his own abilities with architectural space to his descent from a long lineage of coppersmiths: "All these generations of people concerned with space give a preparation. The smith is a man who can make a volume from a flat sheet. Before he begins his task he must have visualized space."[83] The majority of Gaudí's comments are rich and thought-provoking—he was a ready conversationalist and a born teacher. As a well-educated man he was prepared to converse with visiting intellectuals on many subjects.[84] His remarks deserve translation and study, especially those that bear directly on the practice and theory of architecture.

   With regard to his working methods, it should be emphasized that in spite of his improvising and his apparent rule-of-thumb methods, he was not a master mason, but an architect. His associates report that he maintained that dignity that Latins attach to the profession of architect, supervising rather than showing by example. He intervened seldom with his hands, the great exceptions being some of the iron forging and the sculpture that was designed for the Sagrada Familia church. Considering how adept he was with abstract forms and ordinary architectural ornament, we are unprepared for the dismal figure sculpture of the Nativity facade. His first error would seem to be his quite modern belief that the architect should control every detail, which encouraged him to try to train his own sculptors. The second was his commitment to a naturalism so severe that he employed life molds, death masks, dissections, photographs, and even simultaneous reflections from multiple mirrors in order to obtain exact copies of the original.[85]

But it was just this conscientiousness over each detail that accounted for his outstanding contributions to the Catalan crafts revival of his day. No medium was too lowly for him to take on. He was proud to design banners for civic processions (fig. 15, page 31). He moved freely from ceramics to stained glass to ironwork to furniture design. His furniture, as we have seen, is basic to any understanding of Gaudí's work; as with his ironwork he tried to vitalize the ordinary nineteenth-century product by injecting a brisk effect of life and nature. Fortunately Barcelona had developed a number of first-rate shops of craftsmen who could carry out the designs of Gaudí and other Renaixença artists.

In brief summary, Gaudí's furnishings moved from his free interpretation of the medieval which we have observed in the work for Comillas (plates 96–99) to the lively insect-like constructions that he employed for the Casa Batlló (plate 83) or in the Colonia Güell crypt (plate 57). This development is epitomized by the difference between the standing candelabrum designed for the Sagrada Familia (plate 103) and a small candlestick for the Casa Batlló (plate 104). The one is a spikey medieval thing, full of motion and space, but still insistently iron. The material of the second, not identifiable with certainty, has been molded into an image of generalized organic growth. There is a madness here that Gaudí shared with a number of Modernista designers.[87] Some of this spirit he had developed independently well before Art Nouveau came along. As examples we illustrate two pieces which are still today to be found in the Palacio Güell (plates 100–102). As he worked with crews of specialists on some buildings, there are variations to be noticed in style. For instance, most of the furniture for the Palacio Güell was done more conservatively,[88] and the suite for the owner of the Casa Calvet[89] was much less spirited than the sets that Gaudí designed for the business offices on the ground floor (plates 105–107).

Catalan craftsmanship of the period is noted for extravagance of effect, and Gaudí's was no exception. Where possible, as in the Palacio Güell, he made his walls of polished marbles or rich incrustations, but for patrons of more modest circumstances such as the Teresianas (plates 45–50) he produced a polychromy with inexpensive tile and brick. The colorful tiles he designed and used were a mass-produced substitute for costly sculptured decorations on the exterior of buildings. But it is the ironwork of the exterior, like the furniture inside, that lends his buildings a sense of animation even when they are deserted. The techniques vary in his metalwork, and the range of forms is immense; his contributions to this venerable Spanish specialty have frequently been noted.[90]

EVALUATION

THE IMPACT of a creative personality like Gaudí's on his contemporaries and on subsequent generations makes an instructive study.

We should realize, to begin with, that Gaudí employed a quantity of architects, artists in their own right, who served him unstintingly.[91] Of the younger of these, many are still alive today and can testify to the power of his personality and to his effectiveness as a teacher.[92] The manner in which collaborators of the master were engulfed by his dominating personality has led later to acrimonious charges of plagiarism, much as occured among the Oak Park associates of Frank Lloyd Wright. This broke into the open in 1928–29 in the form of a long polemic over Francisco Berenguer—whether he had been exploited by Gaudí and just what Gaudí's buildings owed to his designs.[93] A glance at Berenguer's independently executed commissions, which are mostly distinct from Gaudí's and generally inferior, indicates that Berenguer could not have been the inventor of Gaudí's "decorative system" as was charged.

The type of exchange that may have occurred between Gaudí and other major architects of the Renaixença in their maturity has not, apparently, been studied.[94] The isolation of his later years suggests that Gaudí was not their debtor; he was, in fact, isolated by his own volition from the Association of Architects and received much more attention from young students of architecture than from their elders.[95] As for the practitioners of Modernismo —they operated much more under the sway of France, Germany and Vienna than of Gaudí, whose forms were the most independent of foreign influence in that epoch. The number of buildings that might be called adaptations of Gaudí's seem to be few and rather painful;[96] none of his contemporaries, even the greatest, seem to have possessed that innate sense of unity by which Gaudí made his elements "fit"—structure, geometry and the richest decorative outbursts. To judge from their own reports, the impact of Gaudí on his co-workers was less that of specific architectural elements than that of his personality, his religious faith and his sincere belief in architecture as a way of life.

Gaudí's influence outside of Spain during his lifetime seems to have been nil. It is not clear whether the German expressionist architects were aware of his buildings, although in certain cases the resemblances are striking: e.g., between the windows of Eric Mendelsohn's Einstein Tower and those of the Casa Milá mansard.

Following Gaudí's death his influence as an architect dwindled away even in Catalonia, which is what one might expect if it is true that since about 1910 his major effect has been the personal one of teacher and sage. On the occasion of his demise there was a considerable outburst of writing about him which continued for a year or so, stimulated by the exposition that marked the first anniversary of his death (see Chronol., 1927, p. 32) and by the publication of monographs in 1928 and 1929. A survey of the literature appearing on him reveals that from then on until the late 1940s he received relatively scant attention.[97] Reviews of the 1927 exhibition already revealed considerable disenchantment with his work at that time.

Yet there have always been some groups concerned with him. There is, after all, the cult of the Sagrada Familia.[98] And Gaudí himself is the center of a cult. In Barcelona he is an institution: every Catalan feels strongly about him, pro or con, as an American feels about a baseball team, and even the "cons" are agreed that he was a genius. When in 1952 a scholar in Madrid dared question this, he set off an outburst from piqued Catalans that continued in the press for more than four months.[99] Another group of interested individuals comprises the startled tourists and itinerant photographers who write feature articles about his Barcelona buildings upon their return home.

Within the arts, it was mainly the Surrealists who kept his memory alive. Salvador Dalí, his compatriot, published dramatic photographs of his buildings in 1933[100] which brought

Gaudí to the attention of the *avant garde* during the years when most architects were unconcerned or hostile to him.[101] An interest such as the Surrealists' in the suggestive meanings of Gaudí's forms still persists, but in recent years the craftsmen and other segments of the artistic world have become intrigued with him. It is no coincidence that the postwar interest in Gaudí here in America accompanied the rise of our own school of abstract expressionism in painting and sculpture (cf. plate 2). Here was an artist, practicing the collective, businesslike and generally unwieldly art of architecture, and doing so with that same free-wheeling, apparently anarchic individuality that characterized their own style of painting! Between them the Surrealists and the abstract expressionists accounted for a whole new taste in Gaudí-photography that emphasized the painterly or sculptural values of his forms and of his decorative details.

But today one notices that more and more *architects* and *engineers* are visiting Barcelona to look over his buildings. Attention is shifting from the surfaces, textures and forms to the dramatic structure and elusive spatial effects of Gaudí's architecture. Engineers find here their newest pet—the hyperbolic paraboloid surface; architects sense a release from the flattish rectangular shapes that they had come to think were the expression of our machine age. Had not their prophet Louis Sullivan called the Sagrada Familia church, "the greatest piece of creative architecture in the last twenty-five years," saying, "It is spirit symbolized in stone!"[102]

The art of Antonio Gaudí is not easily reducible to the scope of a book or a photograph, even in color. More than most architecture his must be experienced in person. Works like the Park Güell or the Colonia Güell chapel are capable of being savored like an old master painting—after many visits and long contemplation, the spectator notices with delight newly-discovered "passages" of structure or texture. But can such continual surprises and lasting enjoyment be attained generally in architecture today within the conditions that contemporary technology has imposed upon our builders? That is what the engineer, architect and artist ask, and are seeking to answer for themselves there in Barcelona.

The Notes to the Text begin on page 122.

CHRONOLOGY OF LIFE AND WORKS[103]

1852 Born Reus (?), June 25.[104]

1867–68 Illustrations for a handwritten school magazine *El Arlequín* (Reus). No copies seem to have survived.[105]

1869–70 Illustrations for a project for the restoration of the monastery of Poblet.[106]

1874–78 Attended the Escuela Superior de Arquitectura of Barcelona.[107] A number of his student projects are listed and illustrated in Ráfols 1929, pp. 14–19, 267, but these appear to have been lost in the destruction of Gaudí's workshop in 1936. Little information survives about a series of writings on the esthetics of architecture which he composed between 1876–78.[107a]

1870's Collaboration with the architects Juan Martorell and Emilio Sala of Barcelona.

1875?–77 Collaboration as a student with the architect Francisco de Paula del Villar y Lozano in construction of the *camarín* of the Virgin in the Monastery of Montserrat.[21] Illustrated in Ráfols 1929, p. 13. The *camarín*, a peculiarly Spanish type of lady chapel here contains the ancient image of the Virgin of Montserrat.

1876   Collaboration as a student with the engineer José Serramalera in various projects (disappeared) and drafting for the firm Padrós i Borràs (industrial machinery).

1877–82   Works, mainly in collaboration with the *maestro de obras* José Fontseré, in and about the Parque de la Ciudadela of Barcelona.[22] These include the monumental cascade, 1877–82 (plate 9), the balustrade surrounding the monument to Aribau, 1878 (illustrated in Ráfols 1929, p. 13), decorations of the Salón de San Juan, (figure 10), and some details on the entrance gates of the park.

FIGURE 10.

1878   Own writing desk. Preparatory drawing and photograph in Ráfols 1929, p. 225.

1878   Final examinations (January 4) and title as architect (March 15).

1878   Won municipal competition for design of street lights that are now in the Plaza Real of Barcelona. Illustrated in Ráfols 1929, p. 22.

1878   Furniture for Juan Martorell's pantheon-chapel for the first Marqués of Comillas in Comillas near Santander (plates 96–99).[27]

1878   Design for Church Monstrance. Drawing is in Municipal Museum of Reus (figure 11).

1878   Glass show case for the glove-maker Esteban Comella at the Paris Exposition. A tiny drawing for this on the back of his business card still exists in the Municipal Museum of Reus. Illustrated in Ráfols, 1929, p. 22.

1878–80   House of Manuel Vicens, now 24–26 calle de las Carolinas, Barcelona (plates 10–12). The original condition of the house is illustrated in Ráfols 1929, pp. 27–36, and in Bergós 1954, p. 69. The house, grounds, and enclosing fence were greatly enlarged and modified in 1925–26 by the architect J. B. de Serra Martínez, a friend of Gaudí working under Gaudí's instructions. De Serra's work received the annual prize of the Ayuntamiento.

1878–82   Constructed a machinery shed (fig. 1) and kiosk (fig. 12) and designed workers' housing and other buildings for the textile cooperative "La Obrera Mataronense" in Mataró, NE of Barcelona.[9]

1879   Drawings for an allegorical cavalcade in Vallfogona de Riucorp (east of Lérida). These drawings, partly illustrated in Ráfols 1929, p. 20, are today in the Municipal Museum of Reus.

1880   Street lights for the Paseo Nacional on the Barceloneta waterfront in Barcelona. Similar to those of the Plaza Real (above), only two seem to have survived, at the entrance of the Paseo.

FIGURE 11.

1880   Collaborated with the engineer Serramalera in a project for the electric illumination of the Muralla de Mar waterfront of Barcelona, which was not carried out. Illustrated in Ráfols 1929, pp. 14–16.

1880–82   Altar and benches for the chapel of the Colegio de Jesús-María, calle Méndez-Núñez, Tarragona. Seem to have disappeared. Illustrated in Ráfols 1929, p. 37.

1882   Entered into the dispute over the completion of the facade of the Cathedral of Barcelona, making a rendering of Juan Martorell's (unsuccessful) project that has been variously published.[108] See figure 25 on page 131.

1882   Project (unexecuted) for a hunting pavilion for Eusebio Güell at Garraf (SW of Barcelona). Illustrated in Ráfols 1929, p. 26.

1883–85   Summer house for Máximo Díaz de Quijano, son-in-law of the first Marqués of Comillas at Comillas near Santander (plates 1, 13, 14). Work was actually supervised by architect Cristóbal Cascante.[33]

1883   Project for an altar at Alella, NE of Barcelona (plate 15).

1884   Undertook works of the Expiatory Church of the Holy Family in Barcelona, succeeding Francisco de Paula del Villar y Lozano.[109] One of Gaudí's

FIGURE 12.

FIGURE 13.

FIGURE 14.

first drawings for the building is illustrated in figure 13. The chronology of the works of this, his major building, is as follows:

1875 Original project, a replica of Loreto in Italy. No architect engaged.

1882 Simple neo-Gothic designs by del Villar, the diocesan architect (figures 2a, b).[37]

1882–91 Construction of crypt, which it appears was vaulted by 1887.

1884 Gaudí's project for chapel of S. José in the crypt (figure 14). Mass was celebrated here from 19 March 1885, before the crypt was vaulted.

1887–93 Apse walls and finials constructed.

1891–1903 Portals and structures adjoining the Nativity transept facade erected (plates 16, 17, 19).

1903–30 Work on towers of Nativity transept. A successful carillon test was made in 1915; masonry work of the first tower was completed in April 1918; the first spire was entirely finished in December 1926, the others following in 1927, 1929, and 1930 (plates 7, 16, 18).

Plans for the lantern of the crossing were completed about 1910, for the Chapel of the Assumption and for the main (Gloria) facade about 1916, for the other (Passion) transept about 1917 (plate 20). None have been carried out.[80] Preparatory drawings for these and other elements of the church are illustrated in Ráfols 1929 and Puig Boada *S.F.* 1952.

1885 Altar of the private oratory of house of José M. Bocabella, 31 calle Ausias March, Barcelona. Dismantled in 1936. Illustrated in Ráfols 1929, p. 41.

1885–89 "Palacio Güell," a mansion for Eusebio Güell y Bacigalupi, 3 & 5 calle Conde de Asalto, Barcelona (plates 27–38, 100–102). Ceded to the city in 1945, the building has served as headquarters of the Amigos de Gaudí since 1952, and also as Museum of the Theatre since 1954.

1887 Work on the Güell estate, "Finca Güell," in Las Corts de Sarriá, a suburb of Barcelona. This included construction of the extant gatehouse and stables on the Avenida de la Victoria (plates 2, 39, 40); modifications to the main house, which were later lost when it was converted into a Royal Palace (a roof terrace of this is illustrated in Ráfols 1929, p. 25); construction of walls and another entrance gate which were later destroyed (illustrated in Ráfols 1929, pp. 52–53).[34]

1887 Trip to Andalusia and Morocco with second Marqués of Comillas.

1887–93 Work on the Episcopal Palace in Astorga for Bishop Juan Bautista Grau. This stopped and Gaudí's designs were abandoned with death of the Bishop in 1893. In 1905 work was resumed by architect Luis de Guereta, who finally roofed building in 1907. Interior is still under construction (figure 3, plates 41–43).[48]

1888 Pavilion of the Compañía Trasatlántica (for the Marqués of Comillas) in the Exposición Universal in Barcelona. Illustrated in Ráfols 1952, p. 16.

1889–94 Colegio de Santa Teresa de Jesús, 41 calle Ganduxer, Barcelona, for Enrique de Ossó, founder of the Order (plates 45–50).

1891–94 "Casa de los Botines," a business and apartment building constructed on the Plaza de San Marcelo, León, for the partners José and Aquilino Fernández Riu and Mariano Andrés Luna (figure 4, plates 51–53).[110] Its popular name derives from the founder of their firm, Juan Hons y Botines. In 1954–55 its lower floors were modified by the bank which has owned it for thirty years.

1892–93 Project for a Spanish Franciscan mission in Tangier, designed on commission for the Marqués of Comillas (plate 44).[35] Unexecuted.

1898–1904 House for the sons of Pedro Mártir Calvet, 48 calle Caspe, Barcelona. Most of the work had been finished in 1899 as the inscription on the cornice indicates. In 1900 this building received the first annual prize of the Ayuntamiento of Barcelona (plates 54, 55, 105–107).[59]

1898–1915 Work on the chapel for the Colonia Güell (a textile workers' settlement) at Santa Coloma de Cervelló (just west of Barcelona). Although planning began in 1898, construction started only in October 1908, and Gaudí seems to have relinquished the work to his assistant Francisco Berenguer in 1913. The crypt, the only part to be finished, was inaugurated in November 1915 (figure 9, plates 5, 56–63). Berenguer constructed a number of other buildings throughout the community.[78]

c. 1900 Banner for the choral society of San Feliu de Codines, north of Barcelona (figure 15). This was first mentioned in *Destino* (Barcelona), 28 Oct. 1950.

1900 Designs for modification of the exterior of the Sanctuary of the Misericordia of Reus. The drawings are in the Municipal Museum of Reus (figure 16).

1900–1902 "Bell Esguard," a villa for the Figueras family in the Barcelona suburb of Bonanova, constructed on the ruins of the ancient country house of King Martin I, "el Humano" of Aragon (plates 4, 64, 65).[50] Some of the decoration of the entrance was done by Gaudí's assistant Domingo Sugrañes.

FIGURE 15.

1900–14 "Park" Güell, a garden suburb laid out for Eusebio Güell on the slopes of Montaña Pelada (Monte Carmelo) above the center of Barcelona (figure 5, plates 3, 66–71). Unsuccessful as a housing development, it has for many years been a municipal park. Gaudí lived there from 1906 until shortly before his death in 1926. His own structural drawings for the inclined piers of the Park viaducts are illustrated in Ráfols 1929, pp. 152–53.

1901–02 Wall and gate of the *finca* (estate) of Hermenegildo Miralles on the Paseo de Manuel Girona in Las Corts de Sarriá suburb of Barcelona. The Miralles house and all decorative details except the wall and gate were executed by his assistant Sugrañes (plates 72, 73).

1904 House plans for Luis Graner, 40 calle nueva de Santa Eulalia, Barcelona. Only the fence and foundations were begun, and they have disappeared. His sketches are in Ráfols 1929, pp. 171–72. A bridge over the adjacent Pomeret gully was to have been constructed with inclined supports like the Park Güell viaducts. The drawings for it were lost in Gaudí's workshop in 1936.

FIGURE 16.

1904 Project for the Primer Misterio Glorioso of the Rosary groups on the mountain at Montserrat. Gaudí's drawing for this survives only in a poor newspaper photograph of uncertain date (figure 17). Only one sculpture was carried out under Gaudí's direction. His work there is described in *Templo* XCI (Feb. 1956).

1904–14 Interior reform of the Cathedral of Palma de Mallorca.[73] Unfinished. The type of change made by Gaudí in order to restore the interior to its original medieval condition and to make possible a more open, modern liturgy includes the following: Moved choir and its accompanying furniture from the nave to the sanctuary; freed altar by removing various *retablo* elements to side walls of the building; placed episcopal chair in full view of congregation; designed a hanging baldachin of iron and a series of iron lighting fixtures, hanging and attached, throughout the interior; opened windows that had been blocked and designed stained glass for them;[111] designed a number of sculptures and relocated others; prepared models for the royal tombs (figure 18).

FIGURE 17.

1905? Pulpits for the parochial church in Blanes (near Gerona) (plate 74).[112]

1905–07 Remodeling of building at 43 Paseo de Gracia, Barcelona, for the Batlló family. Popularly called "Casa de los huesos." All exterior surfaces were redesigned: front and rear facades, roof and light well. However, the only

31

interiors which he seems to have decorated were the ground floor, principal floor, and attic (plates 8, 75–85, 104).

1905–10   Building for Doña Rosario Segimon de Milá (called "La Pedrera") at 92 Paseo de Gracia (corner of calle Provenza). Although demolition work began in 1905, Gaudí's plans were not ready until February of 1906. These plans bore only the vaguest relation to the final appearance of the building (cf. plates 86, 87). Construction proceeded slowly owing to many changes in plan and infractions of the building code. Following a dispute with the proprietor in 1909, Gaudí seems to have left the termination of the work, i.e., interior and exterior decoration, to his assistant José M. Jujol. A number of Gaudí's ideas, such as the Madonna statue on the roof and the tiling of the patio walls, were not carried out. The patio walls were painted in imitation of tapestries under the direction of Alejo Clapés (figures 6, 7; plates 6, 86–94).

In 1954 the garret was made into a series of modern duplex apartments by the architect F. J. Barba Corsini, and a number of smaller chimneys were added to the group on the roof. This modification is illustrated in *Cuadernos de Arquitectura* no. 22 (1955). Measured drawings of three of Gaudí's floors were published in *Cuadernos* no. 26 (1956).

FIGURE 18.

1908   Various projects for restoration of the Barrio Gótico of Barcelona. These were sketched in on photographs and postcards. Of a monument to Jaime el Conquistador he seems to have executed only some painted phrases on old walls in the calle Tapinería (figure 19).[113]

1909   School building of the Sagrada Familia (figure 8, plate 95).[76]

1910   Exhibition of models, photographs and drawings of Gaudí's work in the Societé Nationale des Beaux-Arts, Paris. This was the most important exhibition of his work during his lifetime.[114]

c. 1910   Gaudí begins to withdraw from all commissions except the Church of the Sagrada Familia (see chronology of his subsequent works there under "1884").[13]

1922   Congreso de Arquitectos de España (Madrid) adopts a motion praising the architect Gaudí.

1926   June 7: Gaudí is struck by a trolley car near the Plaza de Tetuán while on his way from the Sagrada Familia to worship at the church of S. Felipe Neri in the old quarter of Barcelona.

FIGURE 19.

1926   June 10: Gaudí dies in the Hospital of Santa Cruz. He was buried on the 12th in the crypt of the Sagrada Familia.[19]

Posthumous Honors, Expositions, etc:

1926   (December) Memorial lectures on Gaudí and his work in the Cercle Artístic de Sant Lluc, and in the Escuelas de la Sagrada Familia of Barcelona.

1927   (June) Memorial exhibition of photographs and models of Gaudí's work in the Sala Parés of Barcelona.[115]

1952   Centenary celebration of Gaudí's birth.

1952   (January) The "Amigos de Gaudí" founded as a section of the old Cercle Artístic de Sant Lluc.

1952   (September) The City of Barcelona declares all Gaudí's buildings classified as historical monuments.

1952–53   International photographic and essay competitions on Gaudí held by the "Amigos de Gaudí." Essay prize awarded to Dr. Nikolaus Pevsner of England.[116]

1953   (March) Acts in honor of Gaudí by the Colegio Oficial de Arquitectos de Cataluña y Baleares.

The Chronology of Life and Works is continued on page 121.

1. Porch tower of "El Capricho," a summer villa at Comillas on the coast near Santander, 1883–85. (See also plates 13, 14.)

2. "Abstract expressionism" more than a half-century ahead of its time. Detail of the broken-tile surface of a cupola on the stables of the Finca Güell, Barcelona, 1887. (See also plates 39, 40.)

3. Benches of the Park Güell, Barcelona, decorated from about 1908 under Gaudí's direction. By this time his surfaces are warped so irregularly that the use of the usual square Spanish tiles as covering would have been impossible. (See also plates 66–71.)

4. A detail of the wall of "Bell Esguard," Barcelona, 1900–1902, illustrates Gaudí's manner of combining a variety of warm earth-colored stones in a decorative rubble-work. (See also plates 64, 65.)

5. Exterior wall of Colonia Güell chapel. An infinite variety of shapes and tones of the clinker bricks and basalt fragments contrasts with the vivid polychrome of the tiles and colored windows. (See also plates 56–63.)

6. Roof of the Casa Milá, 1905–10. Through the parabolic arch Gaudí planned that we should see his symbol of the new city of Barcelona—the Sagrada Familia church.[40] (See also plates 86–94.)

7. Sagrada Familia church spire, 1920s. Here the curvilinear warped surfaces gave way to flat, angular, shifting planes produced by the complex interlocking of geometric shapes. (See also plates 16–26.)

8. On the upper facade of the Casa Batlló, Barcelona 1905–07, not only are the surfaces iridescent, but they also shift from golden orange to bluish-green in a complex counter-change. (See also plates 75–85.)

9. Cascade in the Park of the Ciudadela (Citadel) in Barcelona constructed with Fontseré 1877–82. An extravaganza such as this has little to commend itself to twentieth-century taste, but as part of a large park layout it served as a good lesson in spatial planning.

10. The Casa Vicens seen from under Gaudí's parabolic brickwork cascade (now destroyed to make way for an apartment house).

11. A section of the wrought and cast iron fence of the Casa Vicens illustrating Gaudí's use of lively plant forms and curved iron work that anticipate the Art Nouveau of the 1890s.[30]

12. Casa Vicens, Barcelona 1878–80, just after its modifications were completed and the street widened in 1925–26. As designed by Gaudí the present entrance door had been a window, and one of the present street windows served as the entrance. There were no grilles on the street windows, and the fence stood about 25 feet in front of the house.

13. View of "El Capricho" at Comillas (Santander) 1883–85. Its bright greens and warm brick hues merge with the vegetation of the family park. Martorell's pantheon-chapel can be seen in the background.[24]

14. Detail of the ceramic and iron work of the tower of "El Capricho." This gallery and the top lookout above it command a spectacular view of the Bay of Biscay, over the town of Comillas in front.

15. Unexecuted project for a neo-Gothic chapel in Alella (northeast of Barcelona). Signed and dated by Gaudí (July 1883), it resembles the chapels that he designed for the crypt of the Sagrada Familia church.

16. Facade of the Nativity of the Templo Expiatorio de la Sagrada Familia in Barcelona, carried out between about 1890 and 1930. It rises from a neo-Gothic base, through Art Nouveau portals to Cubist pinnacles.

17. Detail of the Nativity transept of the Sagrada Familia church and adjacent cloister roofs. An underlying Gothic structure was here overlaid with fluid decorations as his ideas evolved between 1891 and 1903. Some of the figure sculpture is restoration following the destruction of 1936–39.

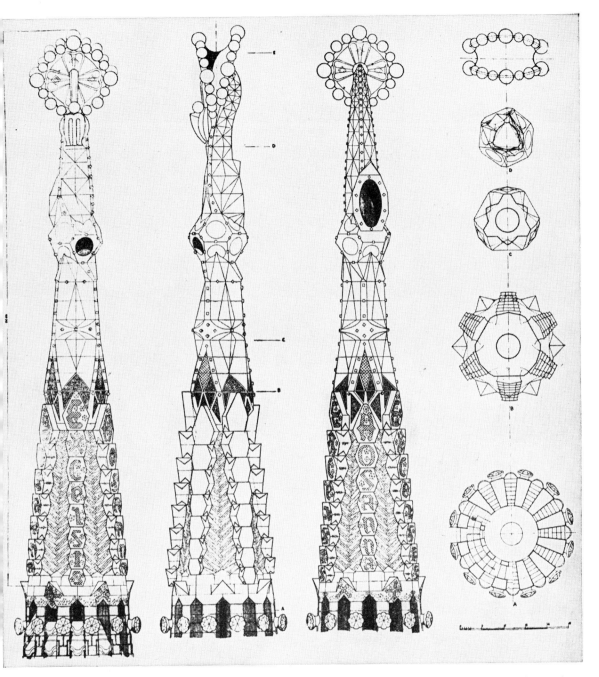

18. Architectural drawing of a pinnacle of the Sagrada Familia church. Front, side and back views with five sections drawn at points A, B, C, D, and E. Note the hole for searchlight installation two-thirds of the way up.

19.   View of the Sagrada Familia church from the side of its unfinished nave—the early Gothic Revival apse can be seen at the left. Note that the church will in time be surrounded by the public parks and gardens that its builders intended.[39]

20. Chalk and ink drawing of 1917 for the other transept of the Sagrada Família church, that of the Passion. It resembles more the Colonia Güell (plate 56) than the earlier transept (plate 16).

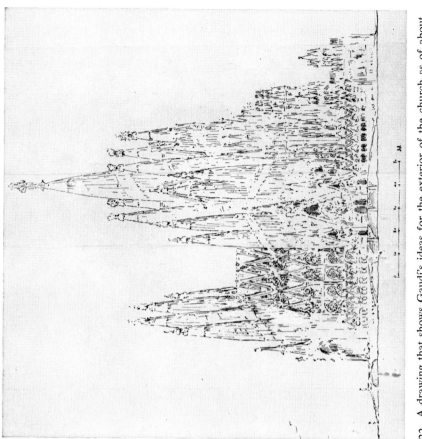

22. A drawing that shows Gaudí's ideas for the exterior of the church as of about 1906. Note that the pinnacles are of a foliated Gothic form, not the final type. (Compare plate 16).

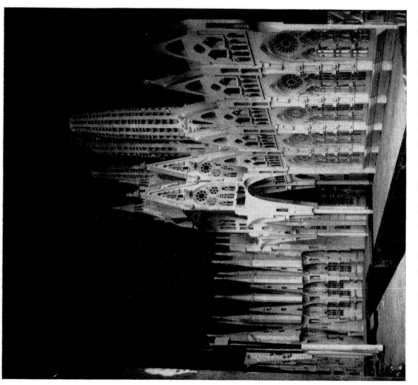

21. Early model for the Sagrada Familia church (c. 1910). This model, employs parabolic arches, but otherwise uses Gothic structure with vertical piers.

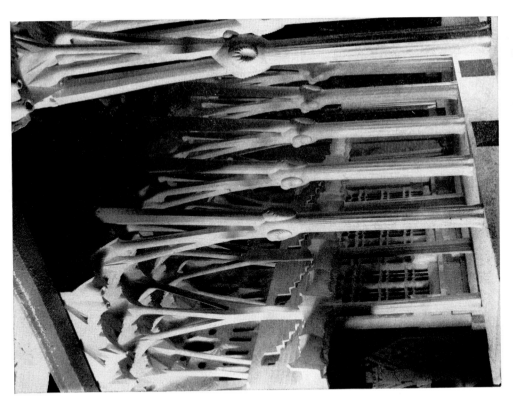

24. Present model for the nave of the church. It uses inclined tree-like supporting piers as well as vault and wall surfaces made of hyperbolic paraboloids that produce attractive star-like patterns. It is based on Gaudí's last model of about 1925 (destroyed).

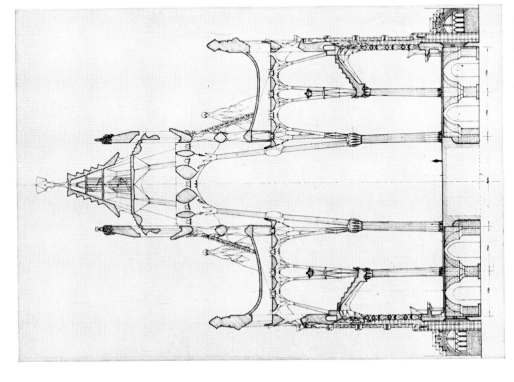

23. Transverse section of the nave of the church of the Sagrada Familia as it is now planned. Here can be seen the structure of the roof, composed of a series of pyramidal units rising more than 75 feet above the vaulted ceiling.

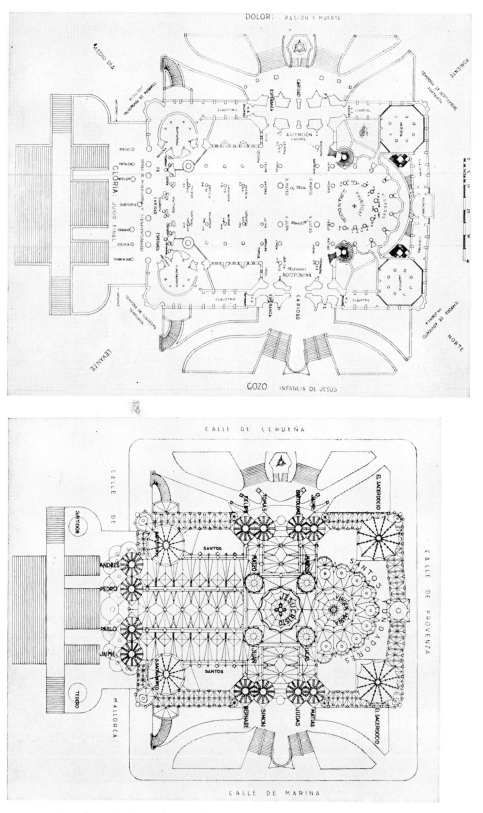

25, 26. Two schematic plans of the projected church of the Sagrada Familia: (25, top) drawn at floor level, shows the liturgical use of the internal parts and explains the symbolism of the piers and portals; (26, bottom) drawn at heights that reveal the different vaulting forms, gives the names of the towers and cupolas.

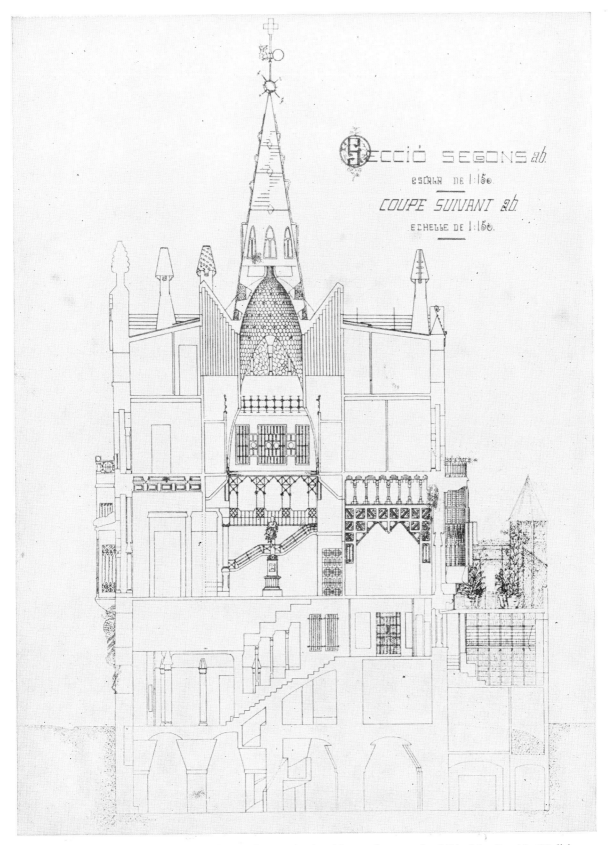

Ecció SEGONS ab.
ESCALA DE 1:150.

COUPE SUIVANT ab.
ECHELLE DE 1:150.

27. A section through the Palacio Güell from front to back. This was drawn and published for Eusebio Güell in connection with the exhibition of Gaudí's works in Paris in 1910.

28. The Palacio Güell (1885–89) is situated in a bohemian quarter of Barcelona just off the Rambla de Capuchinos, which can be seen at the street's end. Picasso once had his studio on a roof opposite.

29. Typical of the painstaking craftsmanship of the Palacio Güell is this three-dimensional construction evolved from the escutcheon of Catalonia. The door grilles are so contrived that one sees out but not in.

30. These parabolic arches were selected by Eusebio Güell over a variety of more conservative facade designs that Gaudí prepared for him. The curling Art Nouveau ironwork of the doors contains the patron's initials "E" and "G" above and at the bottom corners, coiled serpents.

31. Rear of the Palacio Güell. Note how the unusual blinds and the variety of roof elements contrast with the simple rhythms of the window openings.

32. Roof of the Palacio Güell. The tall cupola shell is surmounted by a cross, with which Gaudí nearly always finished off his buildings.

33. Palacio Güell, Barcelona. Entrance vestibule with dismounting steps. Carriages were parked in coachroom behind the door at left. The bulging grille behind the steps gives light to the spiral ramp below.

34. Interior of the Palacio Güell (1885–89) in its heyday. (This is the shuttered bay-window of plate 31). Unfortunately the house was occupied during the Civil War by the garbage-collector's union and stripped almost bare.

35. Palacio Güell, Barcelona. Gaudí's three-dimensional version of what the Spaniards call an "artesonado" ceiling.

36. Palacio Güell, 1885–89. Wrought-iron decoration of an arch in an upper-floor bedroom,

37. In the Palacio Güell's underground stables heavy mushroom columns of brick and flat Catalan tile vaulting support the floor above.

38. The stables in the basement (*śotano*) of the Palacio Güell employ a spiral ramp of brick and of tile for the horses to descend from the coachroom above.

39. Dragon gate of the Finca Güell. One of the most elaborate examples of the wild outburst of iron-work in late 19th century Catalonia. The dangling clains are characteristic of contemporary gates, but the delicate meshwork is unusual.

40. Gatekeeper's lodge of the Finca Güell in Barcelona, 1887. The tall arches, the interlocked brick pattern and the endless repetition of circles in stucco remind one vaguely of Moslem architecture. Notice how simply and economically the designs are worked out with raw building materials.

41. The Episcopal Palace in Astorga, 1887–93. It was Gaudí's desire to construct an edifice appropriate to the harshness of the Spanish meseta and in keeping with the dignity of his friend the Bishop Grau. (Astorga cathedral is behind at the left).

43. Basement of Episcopal Palace of Astorga. Gaudí's underground vaulting is always powerful, complex and Catalan in technique. (**This** now serves as a museum).

42. Entrance to the Astorga Palace. This unusual portal seems to recall, vaguely, ecclesiastical hats, crowns and canopies.

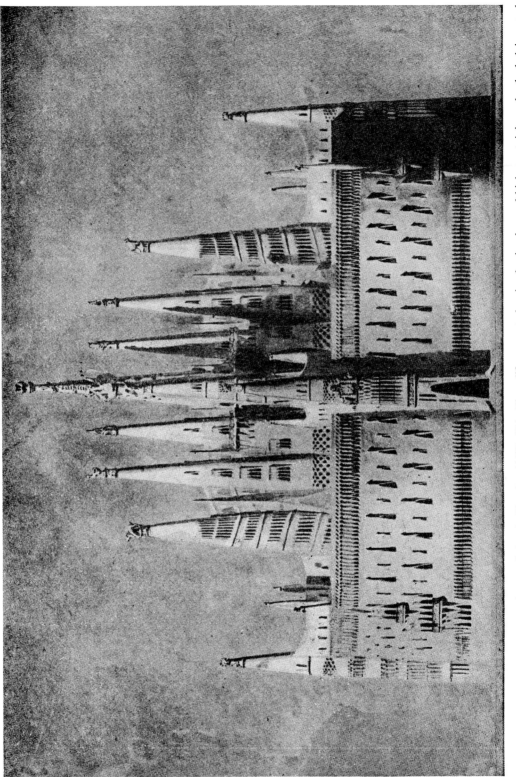

44. Drawing by Gaudí for a Franciscan mission in Tangier (1892–93). The edifice was to be circular in plan and high, containing schools, lodgings and other facilities. In the central compound was to rise a chapel, whose many towers seem to have been the inspiration for later work on the Sagrada Familia church (compare plate 16).

45. Teresan school in Barcelona, 1889–94. These external walls are of rubble interlarded with brick and terracotta ornament. The whole is done in soft earth colors ranging from tan to reddish brown.

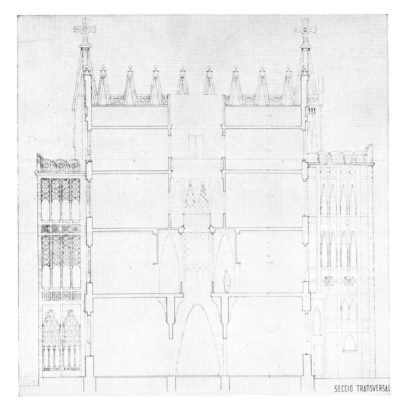

SECCIO TRANSVERSAL

46. Transverse section of the Colegio de Santa Teresa de Jesús drawn for the
architect Luis Bonet y Garí.

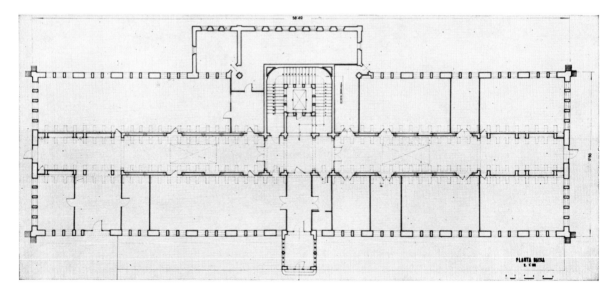

PLANTA BAIXA

47. Plan of the ground floor of the Colegio de Santa Teresa de Jesús drawn for the architect Luis Bonet y Garí.

48. Teresan school entrance gate. This is in the age-old Spanish tradition of *rejas* (grille-work), here spikey like those of León (plate 51).

49. Interior of the ground floor of the Teresan school, 1889–94. Notice how simply and strongly the structural lines of the various arches and piers are articulated. Chicago architects were developing a similar bare rationalism in metal in these same years.

50.   Arcades of the first floor of the Teresan college. Here the piers are only one brick thick. Parabolic arches have by now become standard for Gaudí.

51. Door grille of the Case Fernández-Andrés of León (fabricated in Barcelona) contains the lion of the
city at top. The sculptured St. George of *Barcelona* above caused a stir in León; the present one is a
modern replica of 1956.[110]

Proyecto
(de la Casa
de los
Sres Fernandez y Andres

Alzado.

esc 1:100.

Barcelona Diciembre
1891

Los Propietarios.   El Arquit.

52. Gaudí's original drawing for the elevation of Casa Fernández-Andrés of León, 1891. The building was completed in
     1894.

53. Detail of a carved wooden ceiling in the Casa Fernández-
     Andrés.

54. Casa Calvet in Barcelona, 1898–1904. The owner's name (Pedro Mártir) is symbolized by a transfigured saint's head at the cornice, the center one being Peter Martyr. As usual the building is topped with crosses.

55. Lobby of Casa Calvet. As with the Palacio Güell, one of the outstanding qualities of the building is the costliness and variety of materials—natural and artificial—employed in its decoration.

56. View of the porch of the Colonia Güell chapel (1898, 1908–15). Compare plate 60 in order to see what a small portion of the edifice was constructed.

57. Crypt of the Colonia Güell chapel near Barcelona. The roughness of effect throughout the building is enhanced by the irregular way that these inclined columns are cut. Note the spidery benches.

58. Detail under the porch of the Colonia Güell chapel at Santa Coloma de Cervelló (near Barcelona).

59. Detail of the crypt interior of the Colonial Güell chapel.

60. Rough sketch of projected exterior of the Colonia Güell chapel. This was drawn over an inverted photograph of the working model, like our plate 62.

61. Companion sketch for the interior of the chapel of the Colonia Güell, based on an inverted photograph like plate 63.

63. Inverted photograph of the interior of the funicular model in plate 62 shows calculations for the columns and arches of the structure.

62. Inverted photograph of the funicular model for the Colonia Güell chapel hanging in the workshop beside the building. This represents the sheet-calculations for exterior surfaces.

64.   Casa Figueras in Barcelona, called "Torre Bell Esguard," 1900–02. The mosaic benches (1910) and other details of the entrance were done by a follower of Gaudí.

65. Attic of "Bell Esguard." Here, Gaudí called on the wizardy of his Catalan masons to produce what seems to be pure 'Constructivism.'

66. Panoramic view of part of the Park Güell of Barcelona, 1900–14. The building seen above the right-hand gatehouse is the house in which Gaudí lived from 1906 to 1925.

67. View of the stairway and "market hall" of the Park Güell in about 1908 when the ceramic benches of the playground above were still under construction. In this photograph the lizard fountain is concealed behind the serpent one in the center.

68. Roofs and crowning members of the two gate lodges of the Park Güell. The two perforated pinnacles are actually chimney pots.

69 Playground of the Park Güell in Barcelona. In the distance can be seen the Church of the Sagrada Familia. The patterns in tile mosaics on the benches are a child's delight. (See color in plate 3).

70. A gallery of the Park Güell supporting one of the several viaducts.

71.	One of the galleries of the Park Güell. Note the rough pendant stones in the vault and the reinforcing ribs of iron that weave through them.

72. Gateway, Finca Miralles, 1901–02. The roofing, an ingenious water-shedding device, has now disappeared. The central gate is not by Gaudí.

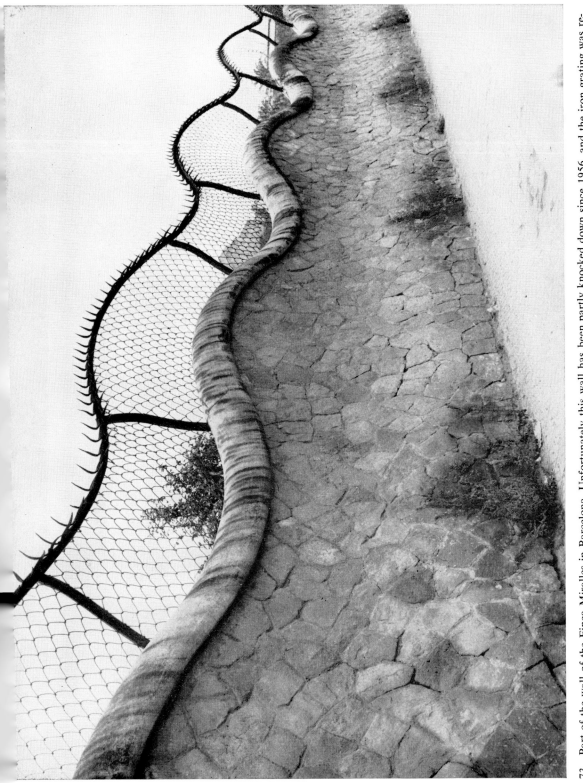

73. Part of the wall of the Finca Miralles in Barcelona. Unfortunately this wall has been partly knocked down since 1956, and the iron grating was removed in 1959.

74. One of a pair of simple pulpits designed for the parochial church of Blanes, near Gerona, about 1905. These pulpits, now lost, were remarkable for their straight lines, which we have seen that Gaudí was inclined to avoid.

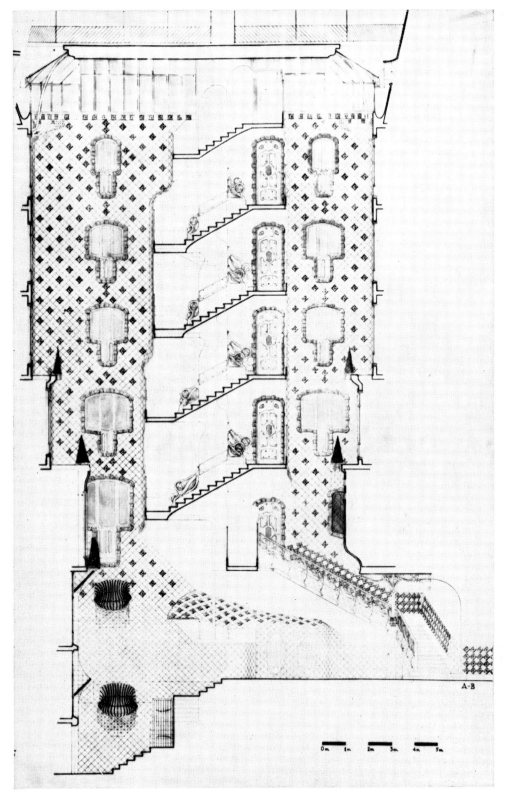

75. Measured drawing of the stairwell of the Casa Batlló of Barcelona drawn for the architect
Luis Bonet y Garí. This court is broader at the top and the tiles are lighter in color at the bottom to ensure illumination of the lower floors.

76. Facade of the Casa Batlló, 1905–07. Adjoining it on the left is the Casa Amatller by Gaudí's friend Puig y Cadafalch.[65] On the cylinder that supports the cross pinnacle are inscribed in gold the initials of the Holy Family.

77. Casa Batlló, facade. In Gaudí's reform of this house on the fashionable Paseo de Gracia of Barcelona the shapes of the original edifice have almost disppeared, especially here below.

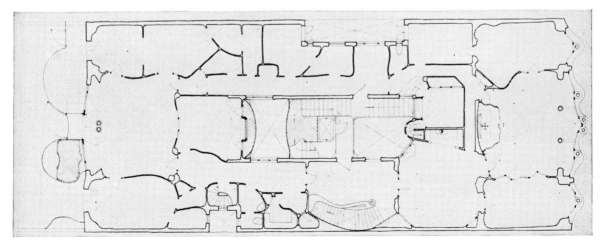

78. Floor plan of the principal apartment of the Casa Batlló as drawn for the architect Luis Bonet y Garí.

79. Entrance vestibule of the Casa Batlló with stairs on the left that ascend to the apartments.

80. View into the skylight that covers the stairwell of the Casa Batlló. As usual, the parabolic arch dominates Gaudí's design.

81. Part of the attic of the Casa Batlló of Barcelona, 1905–07.

82. Entry hall of the principal apartment of the Casa Batlló. Stairway at right comes from the ground level. Gaudí liked small doors that are set in larger hinged panels which can open for state occasions or in order to move furniture.

83. Dining room on the principal floor of the Casa Batlló. Outside of the windows can be seen the terrace garden that goes with this, the owner's apartment

84. Ceramic roofing and pinnacle of the Casa Batlló, 1905–07.

85. Clustered chimney pots of the Casa Batlló present a rather ecclesiastical appearance.

86. Facade of the Casa Milá of Barcelona, 1905–10. The Municipality objected to the pier at the left that juts out into the sidewalk, but backed down when Gaudí threatened to knock the pier out altogether.

87. Gaudí's original drawing for the exterior of the Casa Milá, signed by himself and by the Milás.

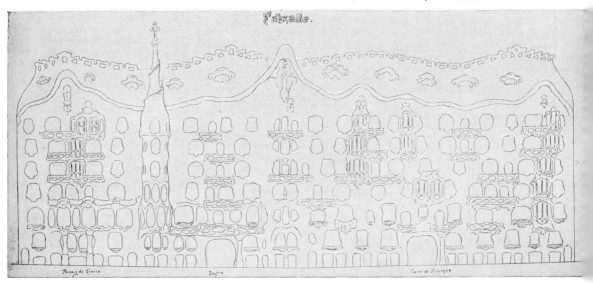

88. Casa Milá. Above the entrance we see the three-part balcony of the proprietor, Doña Rosario Milá, whose monogram ("M" and a rose) appears on the cornice of the building. Her apartment contains more than 20 rooms, most of them large, a private chapel and a theater-salon.

89. Roof of the Casa Milá, Barcelona. The heavy-lidded windows admit light to the inside of the attic vaults (see plate 94). Unlike most of Gaudí's work, the ceramic here is in monochrome of grey, white or tan.

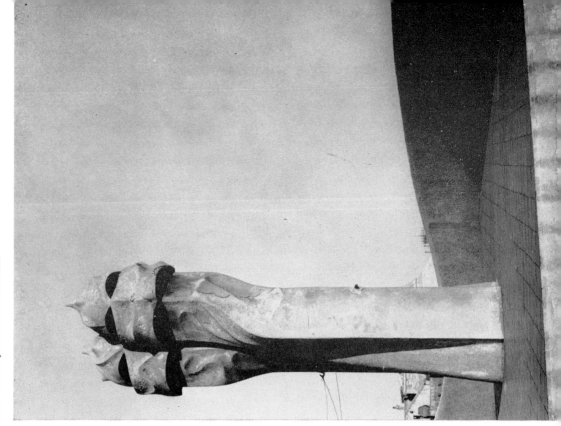

91. Chimneys of the Casa Milá.

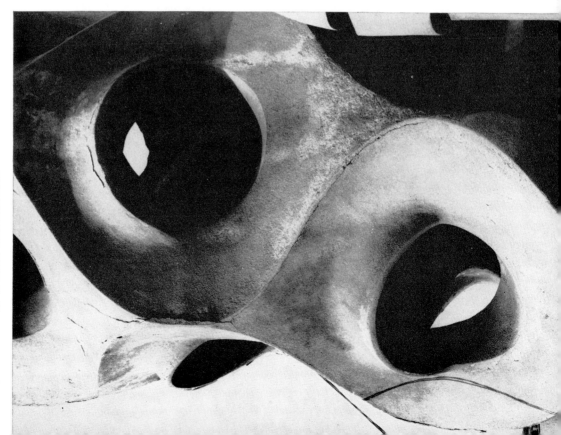

90. Ventilator cover on the Casa Milá roof.

92. One of the two entrance courts of the Casa Milá, 1905–10. Facing us is the grand stairway to the owner's apartment. Beneath us is a subterranean garage (see fig. 7b).

93. An interior of the Casa Milá of Barcelona in the lush days. Gaudí obviously did not decorate this suite, however, this photograph gives some idea of the openness of his planning.

94. The attic (*desván*) of the Casa Milá before it was split up into duplex apartments (1954). Here are the famous Catalan arches and vaults of tiles laid edge to edge, precursors of our contemporary "egg-shell" concrete vaulting.

95. Schools of the Sagrada Familia church, 1909. Gaudi's warped forms were not an artistic affectation, but a simple means of obtaining greater structural efficiency with less material.

96, 97, 98 & 99. Furniture for the chapel of the Marqués of Comillas near Santander, 1878. Out of the medieval repertory Gaudí is

already selecting that which will make his carpentry seem most alive, architectural and spatial in effect.[86]

100. A chaise longue from the Palacio Güell which illustrates Gaudí's early use of the extravagant curvilinear shapes of the Art Nouveau.

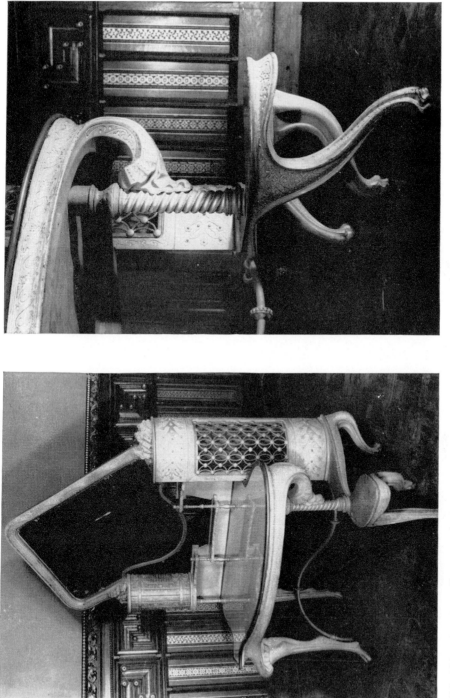

101, 102. An unusually asymetrical and animated dressing table in the Palacio Güell. The lower surface is for lacing shoes.

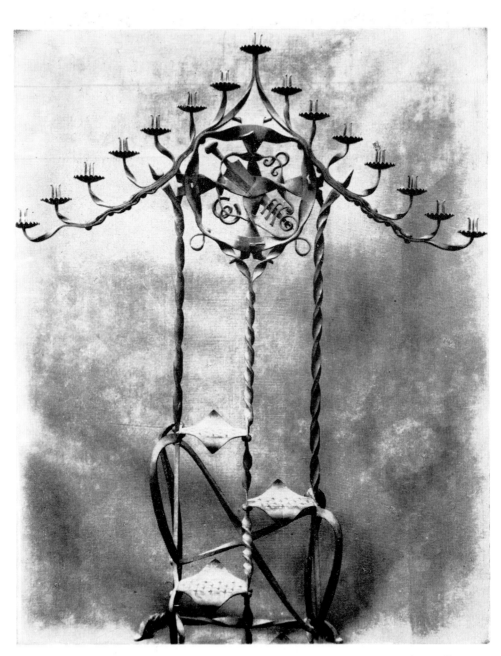

103. Candelabrum designed for the Tenebrae services in the Church of the Sagrada Familia.

104. Detail of the altar of the private chapel in the Casa Batlló.

105. Furniture for meeting room in the business offices of the Casa Calvet, probably about 1901. Curvilinear, robust and ingeniously fit to the human figure.

106. Director's desk in the offices of the Casa Calvet. There is nothing light and fragile about Gaudí's version of the Art Nouveau.

107. Detail of bric-a-brac shelving in
the director's office of the Casa
Calvet (about 1901).

The Chronology of Life and Works is continued from page 32.

1956   (January) Chair of Architecture "Antoni Gaudí" created in the Escuela Superior de Arquitectura of the Universidad de Barcelona.

1956   (June) Exhibition of photographs, models, furniture and metalwork of Gaudí in the Salón del Tinell in Barcelona, organized by "Amigos de Gaudí."

1957   (December) Exhibitions of Gaudí's work open simultaneously in an architectural studio in Milan and in the Museum of Modern Art of New York.

1959   Spanish government sends Gaudí display to the Fifth International Biennial Exhibition in São Paolo, Brazil.

The following works of Gaudí, some of them important, have disappeared, leaving no traces or photographs to indicate their character:

1878   Announcing apparatus, Mataró
1879   Farmacia Gibert, Barcelona
1879–81   Works in Colegio de Jesús-María, San Andrés de Palomar (Barcelona)
1884   Banner for "La Obrera Mataronense," Mataró
1887   Pavilion of Compañía Trasatlántica in Cádiz Exposition
1900   Pilgrimage Banner, Reus (preparatory sketch of a detail illustrated in Ráfols 1929, p. 72).
1901–02   Alterations to Castelldosrius houses, Barcelona
1904   Cinema Sala Mercé, Barcelona

The following works or projects, vaguely referred to by Ráfols and others, have not survived in illustrations:

no date   Studies for a *mirador* (look-out balcony) at Montserrat
no date   Elements of a chapel at Vallgorguina (NE of Barcelona)
no date   Suggestions for a railroad station for Barcelona
no date   Altar at Cervera (west of Barcelona)
no date   Studies for a funerary chapel
no date   Furniture for own house (including dining table of 1885)
no date   Designs for decorations in relief to be manufactured by Casa Miralles of Barcelona, some being used in the former Restaurant Torino, Barcelona, of 1902
no date   Chasuble of metal-thread and pearls for Padre Juan Roquet-Jalmar y Oms of Gerona
1877   Drawings entered in competition sponsored by Ateneo Barcelonés.
1878   Project for a flower stand
1880–81   Drawings entered in competition for San Sebastian casino
1882   Projected church in Villaricos (Almería)
1884   Projected altar in Tarragona
1887   Projected reform of Salón de Ciento, Barcelona
1893   Catafalque for funeral of Bishop Grau of Astorga
1895   Projected tomb for Güell family at Montserrat
1900   Remembrance of his first mass for Mosen Norberto Font y Sagué (some studies for this, in Reus Museum, are illustrated in Ráfols 1929, p. 140)
1908–10   Projected chapel for Colegio de Santa Teresa de Jesús in Barcelona (see chronology 1889–94, p. 30)
1922   Offer of a shrine to the church of the Virgin in Rancagua, Chile.[117]
1923   Studies for chapel and schools for the Colonia Calvet in Torelló (north of Vich)
1924   Pulpit for Valencia

Also Ráfols (1929, p. 271) lists works by assistants in which Gaudí intervened and Cirici *Modernista* (pp. 203–4) illustrates his effect on Juan Busquets' furniture.[118]

121

NOTES

1. Such ideas run through Gaudí's discussions of architectural theory. For him even *structural* forms carried an iconographic meaning, as we observe in his likening of his favorite geometrical surface—the hyperbolic paraboloid—to the Holy Trinity. In speaking to a group of engineering students at the Sagrada Familia church in 1915, he pointed out that the hyperbolic paraboloid is generated by one straight line moving over two others, and maintained that the latter two represent the Father and Son, the moving line being the Holy Spirit which establishes communication between Father and Son (*Diario de Barcelona,* 9 Feb. 1915).

2. See note 82 below, especially Martinell, *op. cit., passim.*

3. All the major books on Gaudí have dealt with this, and in particular two essays: F. Xavier Amorós i Solá, *Presencia de Reus en l'obra de Gaudí* [Reus, 1952]; César Martinell, *La raiz reusense en la obra de Gaudí* [Reus, 1952].

4. The genealogy of the Gaudí family, going back to a merchant of Auvergne in the early seventeenth century, can be found in Bergós 1954, pp. 13–14, 167. Further details are in *El Matí* (Barcelona), 21 June 1936, p. 8; *Diario Español* (Tarragona), 25 Sept. 1951; and *Destino* (Barcelona), 2 August 1952, p. 10.

5. This has been a matter of considerable speculation to his biographers, since Gaudí was prone to discourse on the virtues of married life to his young assistants. There are guarded references to a balked romance, and in "Elogio Preliminar" his friend the writer Maragall wove such a tale about an architect who is presumed to be Gaudí (the writer's son Jordi Maragall confirms this).

Gaudí has been likened to Michelangelo in this respect.

6. Much of our information about Gaudí's youth in Reus comes from his companion Eduardo Toda, who was interviewed by Gaudí's biographers (e.g., "Recuerdos de la infancia y primera joventud de nuestro Gaudí" in *Calendario 1929,* pp. 15–18) and also wrote his own recollections, "Records d'Antoni Gaudí a Reus, fins l'any 1870," *El Matí* (Barcelona) 21 June 1936, pp. 1–2.

7. Although the Academy in Madrid had been giving degrees for architecture for a long time, Barcelona employed the title of *maestro de obras* as awarded by the School of Industrial Arts in the Lonja of Barcelona. In 1869 the Escuela Superior de Arquitectura was established in the Lonja, and during Gaudí's student days it was moved to the new University which was being built by Elías Rogent, first director of the school.

8. His grades in his various schools are reported in Ráfols 1952, p. 187–89, and in Bergós 1954, pp. 15–18, 168. Both authors relate incidents that arose between Gaudí and his instructors. That his attention occasionally wandered is attested to by a page of his Surveying class notes in the Reus Museum that is covered with "doodles," including a rather fine study for a capital (figure 20).

9. La Obrera Mataronense (see Chronol. 1878–82, p. 29) was one of a number of workers' cooperatives that sprang up in Catalonia from mid-century, apparently independent of the English cooperative movement. An idealistic enterprise, it underwent great difficulty, but by the 1870s had obtained a measure of success. Its early years are described interestingly by Joaquín M. Bartrina, "La Sociedad Cooperativa Mataronense," in *Obras en prosa y verso* (Barcelona and Madrid: Texidó y Parera, 1881) pp. 219–58. At the time of World War I it was bought out by an individual proprietor; its buildings are still in use.

10. For an informative discussion of the political situation in which Gaudí was immersed in Catalonia see Gerald Brenan, *The Spanish Labyrinth* (Cambridge: the University Press, 1950) pp. 24 ff. The account is well documented, and there is a general bibliography on pp. 348–9.

11. *Calendario 1927,* p. 27; and Martinell, *Gaudí i la Sagrada Familia,* p. 165, n. 43.

12. Sebastian Kneipp (1821–97), a German monk, devised the system to overcome his own youthful infirmities. In 1881 he established a curative center in Wörishofen, publishing books that went through many editions. They were translated into Spanish, and his system seems to have achieved great popularity in the Peninsula.

Gaudí's frugal diet is often described (e.g., "Parlant amb el capellà custodí del Temple de la Sagrada Familia, Mossèn Gil Parés," *Catalunya Social* VI, 19 June 1926, pp. 3–4), and his extreme Lenten fasting was the subject of an article by Ricardo Opisso in *Diario de Barcelona,* 24 March 1951.

13. It should be noted here, because it coincided more or less with his withdrawal from commercial practice, that in 1911 he almost succumbed to an attack of undulant fever and retired to the Pyrenees with his physician and friend Dr. Pedro Santaló to convalesce. This episode is always emphasized by his biographers.

14. Being dependent on alms exclusively for support, the works of the Sagrada Familia church were in constant crisis. One such occurred in 1905, at which time the Catalan writer Juan Maragall composed a series of pieces for the press of Barcelona, one of which, "Una gracia de caritat" (*Diario de Barcelona,* 7 Nov. 1905), suggested that Gaudí "go out into the street at midday with hat in hand, asking of all alms for the church." It

later became Gaudí's practice to do so. However, Gaudí himself was poor only because he had distributed his own wealth and inheritances to the Catholic church on the one hand, and to the Mancomunidad de Catalonia on the other, the latter being an act of outright Catalanism (*Calendario 1927,* p. 27).

15. We know something of his library. Among his basic religious texts were *Año cristiano; Misal romano; Ceremonial de obispos;* Prosper L. P. Guéranger, *Année liturgique;* and Thomas à Kempis (according to Puig Boada, *S.F.* 1929, p. 101, and *Diario de Barcelona,* 24 March 1951, p. 17).

Regarding secular books, Ráfols tells us (1929, p. 32) that he had read the following treatises on social problems: A. Böckh, *Economié politique des Athéniens;* L. M. Moreau-Christophe, *Du problème de la misère;* and E. Lavasseur, *Histoire des classes ouvrières en France.* (I am indebted to John N. Waddell, Columbia University reference librarian, for verifying these items.)

Architecturally, Viollet-le-Duc was his bible; one of his few trips outside Catalonia took him to Carcassonne where he was flattered to be mistaken for Viollet-le-Duc himself when he was examining the reconstruction (Ráfols 1929, p. 22). Gaudí of course owned art books and periodicals.

Philosophically he is supposed to have been strongly influenced by his collections of Greek classics (Ráfols 1929, p. 220), Goethe (Paul Linder in *Mar del Sur,* Lima, March-April 1950, *passim*), and Shakespeare (Arturo Llopis in *Templo,* LXXXVI, October 1951, p. 8).

16. To these important Catalan clerics should be added Father de Ossó, founder of the Teresianas (see p. 16), the Bishop Morgades and the Cardinal Casañas of Barcelona and the Jesuit Ignacio Casanovas. Although a layman, José M. Bocabella, co-founder of the association responsible for the Sagrada Familia church, also had a spiritual influence on Gaudí.

17. Among articles attributing saintly virtues to Gaudí one might list: Manuel Trens, "L'arquitect de Déu," *La Publicitat* (Barcelona) 11 June 1926; José M. Gich, "Era un sant. . . !," *Catalunya Social* VI (19 June 1926); J. Martí Matlleu, "Un cristiano exemplar: Don Antonio Gaudí," *Almanaque de las conferencias de San Vicente de Paul* (Barcelona: Ormiga, 1927), pp. 82–86; and Octavio Saltor, "Vida para Dios: Antonio Gaudí, arquitecto del Señor," *San José Oriol,* IX Barcelona (May 1956).

18. I. Bückmann, "Antoni Gaudí: Ein pathographischer Versuch, zugleich ein Beitrag zur Genese des Genieruhms," *Zeit. f. d. gesamte Neurologie und Psychiatrie,* CXXXIX (1932), pp. 133–157. Actually this is little more than an enumeration of the well-known events of Gaudí's life plus a few hackneyed efforts to point up psychoses in his behavior. The weaknesses of the analysis were the subject of an entertaining review by Oliver Brachfeld, "Una patografía d'Antoni Gaudí," in *Mirador,* Barcelona (6 April 1933).

19. The quantity of newspaper and magazine articles dedicated to or provoked by the death and burial of Gaudí is so large that they cannot be enumerated here. An almost hour-by-hour chronicle of the events is to be found in the special number of *El Propagador* for 1 and 15 July 1926. An anthology of short literary pieces

that appeared in the Catalan press was collected in *Antoni Gaudí: La seva vida.* Informative full-page spreads describing the funeral were printed in the Barcelona papers from 13 to 15 June. Important necrologies appeared outside of Catalonia in at least six papers of Madrid, in Milan, Paris, etc.

20. Illustrated in Ráfols 1929, pp. 14–19.

21. A *camarín* is a combination of chapel and dressing room for a cult image (especially for the Virgin) situated behind the altar and usually visible through it.

Francisco de Paula del Villar y Lozano (1828?–1901) was a Murcian active in Barcelona. It may have been through his work with this Gothicizing architect at Montserrat that Gaudí made the contacts that later provided him with so much ecclesiastical building. In his diary (lost) Gaudí claimed credit for the Montserrat design, and later he replaced del Villar as architect of the Sagrada Familia church (see p. 13). According to *Anuario* 1927, p. 58, the elder del Villar was aided in both these projects by his son Francisco de Paula del Villar y Carmona (1860–1926). Del Villar *padre* is the subject of an informative obituary in *Anuario* 1903, pp. 443–46.

22. José Fontseré Mestré (died 1897), *maestro de obras,* had won the competition for the construction of a public park on the site of the Citadel of Barcelona. This hated symbol of the authority of Castille over Catalonia had been almost entirely razed in 1841 and 1868, like the fortifications of many other European cities that had outgrown their old defensive boundaries. Gaudí, still a student, worked out the hydraulic calculations for the Cascade so cleverly that he was given credit for the corresponding course at the School of Architecture, although he had neglected to attend the lectures.

23. In Gaudí's papers. See Ráfols 1929, p. 18, and J. M. Garrut in *Diario de Barcelona,* 5 Sept. 1959, p. 40.

24. Juan Martorell y Montells (1833–1906). His works, principally churches, are too many to list here, but certain of his projects had a direct bearing on Gaudí's career. Gaudí and Doménech y Montaner as young assistants helped him in the controversy over the Cathedral facade (see Chronol. 1882, p. 29 and fig. 25), and it was Martorell who recommended Gaudí as new architect of the Sagrada Familia church (see p. 13). He was apparently assisted by Gaudí with the beginnings of the monastery and church of the Salesas (finished 1885) on the Paseo de San Juan in Barcelona. Here occurred a mutual influence. Gaudí is considered to have used the Salesas interior as a point of departure for certain church projects of his own, while Martorell was probably influenced by Gaudí in employing a polychrome tile and rubble exterior for the Salesas. But perhaps the most fruitful interrelationship came in connection with the group of Catalan-style buildings constructed at Comillas (near Santander) for the Marquéses of Comillas. The first Marqués (see note 27) commissioned a large neo-Gothic palace which Martorell carried out between 1878–90 (figure 21). Beside this, and to have been attached to it by an arcade, Martorell constructed a pantheon-chapel, for which Gaudí was asked to design the furniture (plates 96–99).

FIGURE 21.

In 1883 Martorell started the huge Pontifical Seminary nearby for the Marqués, a work that was finished by Doménech y Montaner. Meanwhile, in 1883–85 next to the chapel, Gaudí designed "El Capricho" for the family (plates 1, 13, 14). These buildings, along with a cemetery and some monuments about the town, form a veritable museum of Catalan Renaixença architecture of 1875–90. A number of the works of Martorell are illustrated in Rogent *Arquitectura* and in *Album Renaixensa.*

25. The career of Luis Doménech y Montaner (1850–1923) paralleled Gaudí's in many ways besides the dates of their lives and the points of contact that have already been enumerated. He was an ardent Catalanist, taking an active political role. His early style of architecture was a medieval revivalism exemplified by the Exposition restaurant of 1888 (now a museum). He shared Gaudí's delight in lush polychromatic effects in brick and vitreous materials, and he produced some of the great monuments of Catalonia's Modernismo period, e.g., the Palacio de la Musica Catalán (1891–1908) built to house the musical society "Orfeo Catalá." The extravagance of this building, inside and out, is indescribable in words—with its many-colored ceramics and mosaics, its transparent glass colonnettes, its flying horses of plaster and its stained glass skylight. However, Doménech was of a more practical disposition than Gaudí. He built in the mode of the time rather than fighting it, and he had the persistence to carry out a number of large institutional commissions such as hospitals and hotels. He was also known as a writer and editor of works on art. His buildings are illustrated in Rogent *Arquitectura, Album Renaixensa,* Cirici *Modernista.* For biographical details see his obituary in *Anuario* 1924, pp. 117–21.

26. Elías Rogent Amat (1821–1897) stimulated the revival of medieval styles, crafts and manners in Catalonia through his archaeological studies and other writings; by his reconstruction of medieval buildings such as the Monastery of Ripoll; and through his position as a teacher. Such a building as the new University of Barcelona which he began in 1859 in the Romanesque vein was, of course, influential. He was an impressive lecturer and was accustomed to deliver scholarly addresses during the collective visits of the Association of Architects to Catalonia's ancient sites. Gaudí regularly attended these excursions and must have been much impressed by that of 27 June 1880 in which Rogent, talking about his favorite site San Cugat del Vallés, stressed the political and social basis of the Middle Ages as a way of life. (Elías Rogent, *San Cugat del Vallés,* 2nd ed. [Barcelona: Lopez Robert, 1880], Gaudí listed as present on p. 5). Rogent's buildings will be found illustrated in his son's book, *Arquitectura Moderna,* and in B. Bassegoda y Amigó, *El arquitecto Elías Rogent* (Barcelonia: Farré y Asensio, 1929).

27. This chapel was constructed by Martorell (see note 24) as a burial place for the family and descendents of Antonio Lopez y Lopez (1817–83), first Marqués of Comillas. The Marqués was a self-made man and a perfect example of the new nineteenth-century aristoc-

racy of Spain. As a youth he had emigrated from Comillas to Andalusia to Cuba to Barcelona, parlaying his small earnings into the Compañía Trasatlántica (Spain's biggest shipping line), a tobacco monopoly, banks and a variety of other enterprises. He was ennobled by Alfonso XII in 1878. He and his son Claudio, the second Marqués, played an important role in Barcelona life and patronized such Catalan artists as Martorell, Gaudí, Doménech y Montaner, the sculptors Vallmitjana, Llimona, etc. The seminary that they had erected facing their palace in Comillas was turned over to the Vatican in what appears to have been a politicoreligious maneuver. The palace still contains a remarkable regional museum, although it was looted during the Civil War.

28. See note 9.

29. Besides Martorell and Doménech y Montaner, already mentioned, a pioneer in the new coloristic brick architecture was José Vilaseca y Casanovas (1848–1910), one-time collaborator with Doménech and a leading architect of the Renaixença. He constructed the triumphal arch for the 1888 Exposition of Barcelona in such materials and is also known for his use of oriental motifs. The Catalans were toying with the same flat, floral Egyptain patterns that attracted Louis Sullivan. Vilaseca had a splendid open touring car decorated in the Egyptain style!

Vilaseca's buildings will be found illustrated in Rogent *Arquitectura, Album Renaixensa* and Cirici *Modernista.* His daughter-in-law, the Señora Escobedo Sanchez, has deposited a collection of his original drawings with the Columbia University archive.

30. (plate 11). Actually this detail is of a sketch of the fence around the corner on the Avenida Principe de Asturias, to which de Serra Martínez extended the enclosure in the reform of the 1920s. It is identical with Gaudí's original bit of iron fence and was apparently produced by the maker of the original, Juan Oñós (see note 91).

31. Conversation with Juan Bautista de Serra Martínez 15 July 1959.

32. Illustrated in Ráfols 1929, p. 26. Later a quantity of building was done at Garraf for the Güells by Francisco Berenguer, Gaudí's closest associate. It consisted of an unusual stone building of triangular section which served as a residence, chapel and warehouse (figure 22), and a gatehouse with brick and remarkable wrought iron work (figure 23). Gaudí admired it (Salvador, *Arquitectura* IX, 1927, p. 10), and it has been frequently mistaken for his own work.

33. Although he was usually fussy about the execution of each detail of his structures, Gaudí in this case sent the plans on and left their execution to the architect Cristóbal Cascante, who supervised much of the Catalan work at Comillas. Apparently the building was never seen by Gaudí nor by most of his biographers, who frequently err in describing it. As it is so little known it might be worth observing that: (1) in the garden there is a small grotto with a ceiling of pendant rocks similar to those which Gaudí later employed in the galleries of the Park Güell (plate 71); and (2) the same tiles

FIGURE 22.

FIGURE 23.

(obviously from Barcelona) had been used at the top corners of the verandah of the Casa Vicens (see plate 12). The ceramics that Doménech used for the seminary and its gateway at Comillas are also to be found decorating a number of buildings in Barcelona.

34. Gaudí's modifications to the Güell house were lost when that part of the estate was turned over by Juan Antonio Güell, son of Eusebio, to the royal family of Spain to make their residence in Barcelona. This appears to have been in accord with the centralist policies of the "Lliga," conservative Catalan party to which Gaudí and his patrons belonged. Of the walls that Gaudí constructed around the estate there exists now only an entrance gate, itself recently reconstructed by the University which occupies much of what was once the Güell estate.

35. This was worked out in great detail and with great beauty, according to his associates. Gaudí had apparently been prevented from preparing it immediately by the pressure of his work on the Sagrada Familia, the Güell palace, the Teresian school, the palace in Astorga, etc. Unfortunately the entire set of drawings was lost in 1936, and we have left only one photograph that had been made previously.

36. The modern cult of St. Joseph was developed under Popes Pius IX and Leo XIII. Pius encouraged his worship in 1847 and 1862, proclaimed him to be a patron of the universal church in 1870; Leo urged the formulation of a theology of Joseph in an encyclical of 1889, dealt with his importance to the family and the worker in his "Annum Sacrum" of 1899. In 1865 the Marist father Joseph Huguet of Saint Foy in Dijon had launched a periodical *Propagateur de la dévotion à Saint Joseph* which came to Bocabella's attention. Worship of St. Joseph in the West started in late medieval times, had flourished in Santa Teresa's day (numbering eight monasteries in Catalonia), but had dwindled by the nineteenth century. Bocabella's association immediately won Papal approval, indulgences, apostolic benedictions, and in 1901 Pope Leo XIII began to return half of their annual donations to the Vatican in order to aid construction of the Sagrada Familia church.

For details of this movement in Spain consult *El Día Gráfico* (Barcelona), 19 Jan. 1915; *Diario de Barcelona,* 19 March 1915; *El Universo* (Madrid) 23 March 1915; *La Vanguardia* (Barcelona) 18 Jan. 1915, 2 Sept. 1921; *Templo* (April–May 1952) pp. 5–6, (Sept. 1954) pp. 6–11, (June 1955) pp. 2–11, (March 1959) pp. 10–11; *Obra Mercedaria* no. 41 (Jan.–March 1955), no. 47 (July–Sept. 1956).

Bocabella was a bookdealer, whose seventeenth-century establishment, Librería Herederos de la Vda. Pla, still serves as headquarters for the Association and its church.

37. The simple structure illustrated here, apparently del Villar's first idea, was often reprinted in *El Propagador*. However, Ráfols 1929, p. 42, shows a more sophisticated design by del Villar, seemingly the one he was carrying out when Gaudí took over from him.

38. A large collection of clippings of this nature is preserved in the archive of the Amigos de Gaudí of Barcelona.

39. Bocabella had said in 1881 on buying the terrain,

"On this site will rise the sumptuous expiatory church of the Holy Family, surrounded by gardens for the recreation and enjoyment of children, and accompanied by Catholic schools and workshops with the object of uplifting those gangs of street urchins who wander about lost, and so to facilitate their moral and physical development" (*La Vanguardia,* 18 Jan. 1915). Gaudí described to a visitor the colony of artisans he envisaged clustered about his church, "from which will rise the noises of work, like the buzzing of bees, toward the sunlit church, a mystical hive . . .," (Marquina in *Art et les Artistes* VI (1908) pp. 520–21). Schools for children were constructed on the site in 1909 (see p. 23).

40. In "Una gracia de caritat," see note 14.

(Plate 6). The towers of the Sagrada Familia church are visible from nearly all of Gaudí's structures, although nowhere so neatly arranged as from the Casa Milá, his last building. There seems to be no question that Gaudí was so paying deference to the church which, as architecture, was to dominate Barcelona religiously, complementing the mountain Tibidabo behind the city. The Tibidabo, whose name means literally "tibi dabo" ("to you I will give," Matt. 4:9), is believed to be the mountain on which the temptation of Christ took place.

41. Herman G. Scheffauer, "Barcelona Builds with Bold Fantasy," *The New York Times Magazine* (21 Nov. 1926), pp. 5, 17. Similar articles are to be found in *The Illustrated London News* for 17 Dec. 1927, 10 March 1928 and 23 Feb. 1929.

42. *Bulletí del Centre Excursionista de Catalunya,* XI (April 1901), p. 108.

43. Marquina, *op. cit.,* p. 518.

44. Cf. Viollet-le-Duc, *Dictionnaire raisonné de l'architecture française du XIe au XVIe siècle* (Paris: Bance, 1854–68) V, pp. 472 ff, "Fleuron."

45. *American Architect and Building News,* Boston, XXXVII (9 July 1892), p. 27; *Decorator and Furnisher,* N.Y., XIX (1892), pp. 145–6, 217, 219. Gaudí's assistant Juan Matamala suggests that Americans became acquainted with the Palace through the delegation that visited the Exposition of 1888 in Barcelona. They were there to help dedicate the monument to Columbus at the foot of the Ramblas, near the Palacio Güell. Eusebio Güell's brother-in-law, the second Marqués of Comillas was a director of the Exposition and undoubtedly showed Americans the richly-marbled rooms of the new palace under construction. The same furniture maker (Francisco Vidal) worked for Gaudí and for the American exhibit at the Exposition.

The only monograph on this building is a short one written by Joseph Puiggarí for the Centre Excursionista de Catalunya in 1894: *Monografia de la Casa Palau y Museu del Excm. Sr. D. Eusebi Güell y Bacigalupi* (Barcelona: "L'Avenç"). Informative articles have been published on the Palace by I. Puig Boada, in *Cuadernos de Arquitectura* (Nov. 1944) and by M. Baldrich and by L. Bonet Garí in *San Jorge,* Barcelona (July 1954).

46. In retaining Gaudí as his architect, Eusebio Güell y Bacigalupi (1846–1918) showed himself to be the most radical and open-handed Maecenas of the Catalan Renaixença. No account books were kept between them, and Gaudí seems never to have lacked

funds during Eusebio's lifetime. The Güell fortune had been established by Eusebio's father Juan Güell y Ferrer (1800-1872) who, like the first Marqués of Comillas, rose from simple beginnings to a position of wealth in the Antilles. On his return to Catalonia he started spinning mills ("Vapor Vell") which exploited recent Catalan inventions; he invested in agriculture, became director of numerous financial enterprises. As a writer and a senator he fought for tariffs, against Castillian opposition, in order to protect the young Catalan industries. He married into a well-known Genoese family, Bacigalupi. Eusebio, a worthy son, administered a variety of enterprises, served in politics, was active in the Catalan movement and patronized the arts. Like his father, Eusebio spoke out for full production and protective tariffs to encourage Spanish industry and to raise the standard of living. By the development of his own suburban properties (Finca Güell, Park Güell, etc.) Eusebio tried to direct the expansion of Barcelona into rational, modern form. He was made *gentilhombre del Rey* in 1884, count in 1910. Through marriage or by their own exploits (including heroism), the Güells came into more aristocratic titles than we can list, their relatives *de Comillas* and *de Castelldosrius* being also patrons of Gaudí.

The following may be consulted for biographical information on the family: José de Argullol y Serra, *Biografía del Excmo. Sr. D. Juan Güell y Ferrer* (Barcelona: Succesores de Ramirez, 1881); P. Miquel d'Esplugues, *El Primer Comte de Güell* (Barcelona: Poncell, 1921); P. Rodón i Amigó, *Eusebi Güell industrial* (Badalona: "Cataluña Textil," 1935); Pedro Gual Villalbí, *Biografía de Eusebio Güell y Bacigalupi* (Barcelona: Vélez, 1953); José M. Pi y Suñer, *Gaudí y la Familia Güell* (Barcelona: Amigos de Gaudí, 1958).

47. Salvador, *op. cit.,* p. 16.

48. Useful articles on the Astorga palace include: Amós Salvador, "Gaudí (Impresión de viaje)," *Pequeñas monografías de arte,* Madrid, I (Nov. 1907), pp. 1-4; Angel Salcedo Ruiz, "El Palacio Episcopal de Astorga," *El Universo* (Madrid) XV, 21 June 1914, p. 1; Luis Alonso Luengo, "Gaudí en Astorga," *Revista* (Barcelona) 16 Sept. 1953, p. 14, and 23 Sept. 1953, p. 8 (reprinted in pamphlet form in Astorga, 1954); Enric Casanelles, "Gaudí en Astorga," *Distinción,* Barcelona, no. 16 (Dec. 1957), pp. 69-71.

49. For bibliography on this building see note 110.

50. Gaudí respected the ancient ruins in several ways. The remaining walls he built into a type of terrace in front of the new house. And the access road (now called *calle Bellesguard*) was moved well away to the front, overhanging a gully. This necessitated the construction of a retaining wall and viaduct (figure 24), which he made with inclined piers of rough stone work similar to those of the contemporary Park Güell. Curiously enough, this bit of engineering has passed unnoticed, never having been illustrated in connection with his works.

51. The Park Güell was to be a garden suburb, not a Garden City as has sometimes been suggested; it had none of the means of production that are basic to the latter. However, English Garden City theory was to gain a certain currency in Catalonia later, and Eusebio's son Juan Antonio became president of a civic society that promoted several Garden City developments in that part of Spain. This society discussed the Park Güell in the second number of its magazine *Civitas* (July 1914), praising it, but making clear that it was *not* a Garden City.

52. Drawing for the cross is illustrated in Ráfols 1929, p. 142. The squarish stone crosses standing there today would hardly seem to be connected with Gaudí.

53. *The Secret Life of Salvador Dali* (New York: Dial Press, 1942), caption to plate IV.

54. Regarding Nature and Gaudí's architecture see Joaquín de Entrambasaguas, "Arquitectura y paisage de Gaudí" in *Las manos de la Gioconda* (Valencia: Jeran, 1936), pp. 37-50; James Grady, "Nature and the Art Nouveau," *The Art Bulletin,* XXXVII, no. 3 (Sept. 1955), pp. 187-92; Rafael Benet, "El gust de Gaudí," *La Veu de Catalunya,* 11 June 1928. See also Madsen *Sources* pp. 164-87.

55. For the influence of Goethe in Catalonia see Udo Rukser, *Goethe in der Hispanischen Welt* (Stuttgart: Metzlersche, 1958) and Robert Pageard, *Goethe en España* (Madrid: Consejo Superior, 1958). Gaudí's friend Maragall was influenced by Goethe, translated his works into Catalan and was in great part responsible for his influence in Spain.

In Germany at about this time Rudolf Steiner, a Goethe scholar and occultist, was weaving Goethe's ideas on Nature into a theory of directly expressive architecture that has much in common with the effect of Gaudí's actual buildings.

56. Such as *The Stones of Venice* (London: Smith, Elder, 1851-53) II, chap. VI, paragraphs 67-71. Ruskin had been appreciated by the Renaixença movement for some time and was being translated into Catalan over the year 1900.

57. The only study of the Park Güell is a brief, early one: Salvador Sellés, "El Parque Güell: Memoria descriptiva," in *Anuario* 1903 (also published separately).

58. Not to be confused, as it often was, with the "Modernismo" reform movement in the Catholic church (condemned by Pius X in 1907), which applied historical and comparative methods to the study of religion. Such identification was made in an important contemporary lecture on the "sins" of Modernismo in art: José Doménech y Estapá, "Modernismo arquitectónico," *Memorias de la Real Academia de Ciencias y Artes de Barcelona,* X (March 1912), pp. 55-73. Another characteristically anti-Modernista contemporary view was presented by Lluís María Vidal, "Discurs del Senyor President," *Butletí del Centre Excursionista de Catalunya,* X (Feb. 1900), pp. 32-48.

59. The Calvets were also in the textile business, and this building was constructed in the part of Barcelona where such enterprises are concentrated. Its arrangement of storerooms in the basement and rear, offices on the ground floor, owner's apartment with terrace garden on the first floor and rented apartments above is typical.

Contemporary descriptions of the edifice were printed in Rogent *Arquitectura; Anuario* 1901, pp. 55-63; *Hispania,* Barcelona (15 Dec. 1901) pp. 439-41.

60. The large knocker on the outside door is one of

FIGURE 24.

Gaudí's weirdest bits of iron craft. The heavy open-work knocker, decorated with a cross, on falling strikes the back of a huge louse—undoubtedly illustrating some bit of local folklore. (Illustrated in Ráfols 1929, p. 138).

61. Enrique Sagnier Villavecchia (1858–1931), one of Barcelona's most popular and prolific architects, was, perhaps, most representative of its Art Nouveau phase. He designed brilliantly in that style, but without great conviction, as witnessed by his abandonment of it when the fad had passed. He received many religious commissions, and in 1923 he was titled a Marqués by Pope Pius XI.

Another distinctively Modernista architect was Jerónimo F. Granell Manresa. Both of these men are discussed at length in Cirici *Modernista.*

62. In Rogent *Arquitectura,* p. 151.

The Casa Calvet with its mixture of neo-Baroque and Art Nouveau recalls Horta's Tassel House in Brussels (1892–93), but is less epochal a building, being a conservative pause for Gaudí, while Horta was in a radical phase from which he later retreated.

63. Gaudí was never finicky like Doménech y Montaner or Puig y Cadafalch. His copiers, like Salvador Valeri (Casa Camalat, 442 Diagonal, Barcelona), apply Gaudí's forms as an ornament and never get the building itself into resonance with them. Elsewhere in Spain buildings popularly ascribed to Gaudí can be seen to be no more than a radical version of the Art Nouveau floral style: e.g., in Madrid the Palacio Florestan Aguilar (now Sociedad General de Autores de España), calle Fernando VI, no. 4; and in Bilbao the French Consulate building, Alameda de Recalde 34.

64. It is difficult to evaluate the rock-cut Rosary group designed for Montserrat (1904) in this development, owing to the poor quality of our surviving illustration (figure 17, p. 31). It was to be a shallow grotto excavated in the mountainside in a free and flowing way. The Blanes pulpits, of 1905 (?), are hardly characteristic of his work of the time (plate 74).

65. José Puig y Cadafalch (1869–1956), esteemed Catalan scholar, statesman and architect, was one of the mainstays of the later phase of the Renaixença. He is well known for his publications (Institut d'estudis catalans) on Romanesque architecture and particularly for his theory of the primacy of the Catalan Romanesque. He founded museums, initiated excavations at Ampurias and had time to serve in the Cortes and as President of the Mancomunidad of Catalonia. He designed many buildings in and around Barcelona, all of them rich in tile, ironwork and decorative sculpture, but tending to be derivative of the German Gothic and the Viennese Secession. His was the famous "Casa dels quatre gats" in the old center of Barcelona where the Catalan Modernistas met for beer and Picasso got his start. His works are illustrated in Cirici *Modernista* and in *L'oeuvre de Puig y Cadafalch, architecte* (Barcelona: Parera, 1904).

66. There exists no serious study of the Casa Batlló. However, Jorge Elías gives an amusing account of Gaudí's intransigent attitude toward his clients at that time in "Gaudí y la 'casa de los huesos'," *Diario Español* (Tarragona) 3 Jan. and 4 Feb. 1953.

67. Gaudí's great admirer, the Catalan writer Francesc Pujols, put this nicely: "The wind, the sun and the rain drawn out of heaven in answer to pleadings and prayers, working the stone at the command of Time, are the only ones who can compare with the stonemasons who roughen the stone at the command of Gaudí," in *Revista Nova,* Barcelona, I (23 May 1914), p. 3.

68. One feels that Gaudí's involvement in the wonders of Nature was understandable considering his many associations with the holy mountain of Montserrat, which paradoxically enough serves the Catalans as a center both for religious pilgrimage and for the sport of rock-climbing. The area is also rich in myths of magic rocks and of petrified giants and spirits.

69. Many of the rooms are laid with pale green floor tiles containing marine motifs, which Gaudí designed especially for the building and which are still stocked by their manufacturer in Barcelona.

70. This reaction was stimulated in great part by the writings of the Catalan Eugenio d'Ors, beginning with his essays of 1906. The way in which the classicism of the Greeks, which Gaudí always cited as his model, began to be used against him is cogently described by José Plá, "Gaudí: la Sagrada Familia" in *Grandes Tipos* (Barcelona: Aedos, 1959), a rewrite of essays that had appeared in *Destino* (Barcelona) in Sept.–Oct. 1951.

71. Parisian press comments, puzzled but favorable, are extracted in *Anuario* 1911. Articles also appeared in Italy, Germany and Argentina as a result of the exhibition.

Although Gaudí's retirement of 1910 seems to have come about largely on his own initiative, other events overtook and isolated him by 1914. Probably linked in part to economic crisis brought on by World War I, his work at Mallorca ceased and the patronage of Güell at the Park and at the Colonia Güell was cut off. Eusebio Güell seems to have moved his personal residence from the Güell Palace to his large house (now a school) in the Park Güell, ostensibly for the comfort of his ailing son Claudio. Here he died in 1918 shortly after Claudio. It may be indicative of changed taste on his part that in June 1914 he celebrated the installation in this house of a room of the period of Louis XVI (*La Veu de Catalunya,* 25 June 1914). As regards the Sagrada Familia, in 1914 its *Junta* was badly in debt and wished to suspend the works, Gaudí's only remaining commission. It was at this point that Gaudí and Bocabella's nephew decided to beg for funds. About four years later they received a large donation that permitted construction to continue. Meanwhile Gaudí had occupied himself with calculations and new designs (see Chronol. 1884, p. 30).

72. At a meeting of the *Junta* reported in *Diario de Barcelona,* 24 Dec. 1914.

73. The work at Mallorca, which embraced a good deal of original decoration by Gaudí, has attracted little attention. In style no purist, he was as eager to preserve the Baroque as the medieval, if appropriate to the liturgy. Inventories and discussions of what he did at Mallorca are to be found in Ráfols 1929, pp. 136–44; Bergós 1954, pp. 106–10; M. Rotger, *Restauración de la Catedral de Mallorca* (Palma: Amengual, 1907); Miguel

Alcover, "La Seo de Mallorca y su restauración por D. Antonio Gaudí," *Razón y Fe,* Madrid (10 and 25 June 1928); G. Forteza, "Gaudí i la restauració de la Seu de Mallorca," *El Matí* (Barcelona) 21 June 1936; Pedro Antonio Matheu, *Guías de la Seo de Mallorca: la Capilla Real* (Palma: Pons, 1954); *Idem, Palma de Mallorca monumental* (Madrid: Plus Ultra, 1958); A. Kerrigan, "Gaudí restaurador, ó la historia de Cabrit y Bassa," *Papeles de Son Armadans,* Madrid & Palma, IV (Dec. 1959).

Gaudí did not touch the structure of the cathedral, but did study it, and his assistant there published a memoir on the subject: Juan Rubió Bellver, "Conferencia acerca de los conceptos orgánicos, mecánicos y constructivos de la Catedral de Mallorca," in *Anuario* 1912 (also printed separately).

74. Gaudí's empirical revival of these traditions was paralleled by learned discussions of their structure by his contemporaries in *Anuario,* including José Doménech y Estapá, "La fábrica de ladrillo en la construcción catalana" (1900); Jerónimo Martorell (a friend of Gaudí's), "Estructuras en ladrillo y hierro atirantado en la arquitectura catalana moderna" (1910); and Jaime Bayó (Gaudí's contractor for the Casa Milá), "La bóveda tabicada" (1910).

75. *Anuario* 1916, p. 48.

76. There is no concrete in this building as has sometimes been claimed. The vault is of laminated tiles and tar paper. Gaudí had used the same undulating roof some years before on his neighboring office-studios (now destroyed).

77. A number of explanations of Gaudí's structural innovations exist: Juan Rubió Bellver, "Dificultats per a arribar a la sintesis arquitectónica," in *Anuario* 1913; Domingo Sugrañes, "Disposició estática del Temple de la Sagrada Familia," *Anuario* 1923 (this is the most complete of several articles on the subject by Sugrañes, Gaudí's successor at the Sagrada Familia. This article is reproduced in Ráfols 1929, pp. 172–90, but without the mathematical calculations.); Francesc de P. Quintana, "Les formes guerxes del temple de la Sagrada Familia," *Ciutat i la Casa,* Barcelona (1927) no. 6 (reproduced in Ráfols 1929, pp. 190–203); Juan Bergós, *Materiales y Elementos de Construcción* (Barcelona: Bosch, 1953).

Santiago Rubió, *Cálculo funicular del hormigón armado* (Buenos Aires: Gili, 1952) submits Gaudí's procedures to mathematical proof and extends the system to reinforced concrete.

78. Socially the Colonia Güell also holds interest as a paternalistic but utopian experiment in industrial relations. It was laid out with broad, regular streets, included a school and various social amenities. Its tone was strongly religious, and it was commended by the Pope for its benefits to the working class. Industrially speaking, Güell's associate, the inventor Ferran Alsina i Parellada, was given a free hand. Thumb-nail sketches of the men associated with the enterprise are in P. Rodón i Amigó, *Els Carrers de la Colònia Güell* (Badalona: Museu, 1944).

Technical and historical data on Gaudí's work there can be found in a number of undated booklets on the Colonia Güell, and in Puig Boada, "La iglesia de la Colonia Güell," *Templo,* XCIII (Sept. 1958).

79. A good part of the large bibliography on the Sagrada Familia church concerns itself with the iconography and Gaudí's liturgical planning. Besides the standard biographies, details will be found in the books by Martinell and Puig Boada on the Sagrada Familia and in Manuel González, *Arte y Altar,* 1st edit. (Málaga: El Granito, 1928), 2nd edit. (Palencia: El Granito, 1938).

The books that Gaudí is said to have relied on chiefly for iconography and liturgy are listed in note 15.

80. Work on this transept has recently begun. The church had been badly damaged and its workshops completely gutted in the summer of 1936 at the outbreak of Civil War. The works remained paralyzed until an effort was made to reconstruct the models in 1951. Although Gaudí's drawings were lost and the models smashed in 1936, enough fragments of the models remained for his assistants to reconstruct his intentions (plate 24) and to continue with the building. Since 1955 there has been a big ten-year drive to finish the Passion transept.

But with Gaudí gone the problem arises about how to finish the church. This has led to a controversy among (1) leaving it as he left it, (2) finishing it exactly as he desired, and (3) starting off completely new. The course followed has been essentially (2) and it has been in the hands of his trusted associates, but many feel that as he constantly changed his own plans for it and was considering modifications at the time of his death, there is no present need to adhere to his last plans. There was a considerable polemic about this in the Barcelona papers just after his death, and it has broken out again now that the works have been taken up once more.

81. Marquina, *op. cit.,* p. 522.

82. César Martinell has edited a comprehensive series of conversations which he had noted down as a young student and assistant to Gaudí; his is the most straightforward and systematic collection: *Gaudí i la Sagrada Familia.* Such standard biographies as Ráfols' and Bergós' publish many quotations and anecdotes. Catalan newspapers that reported frequently on the Sagrada Familia works are full of interviews with Gaudí (see p. 13). Prominent visitors to Barcelona like Albert Schweitzer have reported interesting conversations with Gaudí: *Out of My Life and Thought,* trans. by C. T. Campion (New York: Mentor, 1949), pp. 81–82.

83. Martinell, *op. cit.,* p. 134.

84. Gaudí numbered among his devoted friends many of the leading intellectuals of Catalonia. His rejoinders to the king and to important political figures were famous, as were his long discussions with prelates and a dramatic encounter with Miguel Unamuno ("Las líneas rectas del'arquitecto Gaudí" in *El Correo Catalán,* 11 March 1930).

Maragall, the writer, exclaimed, "This man is a poet: on his lips all is truth; all is new; it seems that for him each of his words is a revelation, all that he utters seems to him to be unprecedented, and he delights in it with a joyful surprise, igniting himself in the inspiration of his ardent words. Is this not a poet?," *Forma,* Barcelona, II, no. 16 (1907), p. 25.

85. For descriptions of Gaudí's methods in sculpture

see: Joaquín Folch y Torres, "Arquitecte Gaudí" *Gaseta de les arts,* Barcelona, III (1 July 1926); *idem,* "Gaudí escultor," *Destino* (Barcelona) 11 June 1955, pp. 3–4; A Cirici Pellicer, "La escultura de Gaudí en la Sagrada Familia," *Cuadernos de Arquitectura,* no. 20 (1956), pp. 21–24; Ricardo Opisso, "Las esculturas de la Sagrada Familia," in *Diario de Barcelona,* 5 July 1951, and *Templo,* LXXXVI (July–August 1951); Ráfols 1929, pp. 90–94.

86. (plate 99). These stools, although not previously cited as Gaudí's, seem to be of the same manufacture as the large pieces.

87. This is observable in Cirici *Modernista,* pp. 187–248. The furniture makers of Barcelona responded wildly to the stimulus of the Art Nouveau.

88. The names of most of Gaudí's collaborators in the Palacio Güell are listed in Rogent *Arquitectura,* p. 160.

89. One piece of this Calvet furniture is drawn in Bergós 1954, p. 99.

90. Besides discussions of Gaudí's ironwork in the standard biographies, a series of articles appeared in a special number of *De l'art de la forja,* Barcelona, I (March 1921) dedicated to Gaudí. This periodical was itself a typical product of the Renaixença's interest in the old forges and metalwork of Catalonia. Gaudí's own activities at the forge are described in Ricardo Opisso, "Gaudí: genial maestro de forja," in *Diario de Barcelona,* 2 Dec. 1951 and *Templo* LXXXVII (Oct. 1952). See also Andrés Buil, "Els ferros d' En Gaudí," *La Veu de Catalunya,* 11 June 1928, pp. 4–5.

91. Gaudí's major associates appear to have been the following (no complete study exists of any of these but some information is available on them all in Ráfols 1929 and Ráfols *Diccionario*);

Francisco Berenguer (1866–1914) never became a titled architect, choosing instead to work as a designer for Gaudí and others. His work came closest in stature to Gaudí's own. See notes 32 and 93.

Alejo Clapés (1850–1920) painter who collaborated with Gaudí from the time of the Palacio Güell to that of the Casa Milá.

José María Jujol Gibert (1879–1949), architect, worked largely as a decorator for Gaudí. He did most of the ceramics of the Park Güell and Casa Batlló and the interior and exterior decoration of the Casa Milá. Continued as an independent architect after Gaudí's death. See *Cuadernos de Arquitectura,* no. 13 (1950), pp. 1–22.

Lorenzo Matamala y Pinyol (1856–1927), sculptor, Gaudí's foreman and life-long companion. His son Juan continued with Gaudí (see note 92). Federico Ratera, "Un colaborador de Gaudí: Lorenzo Matamala," *Templo* LXXXIV (Aug.–Sept. 1949).

Carlos Mani Roig (1866–1911), *fin-de-siècle* sculptor who joined Gaudí in work on the Sagrada Familia church about 1907. Ricardo Opisso, "El escultor Carlos Mani en 'La Sagrada Familia'," *Diario de Barcelona,* 30 Aug. 1951, p. 20; Feliu Elías, *Escultura,* II, pp. 128–29.

Juan Oñós, smith in whose shop Gaudí's most elaborate *rejas* were fabricated, including those of the Casa Vicens, Palacio Güell, Finca Güell, León and Casa Calvet. See Opisso "forja," note 90.

Juan Rubió Bellver (1870?–1952), architect whose association with Gaudí included the work in the Cathedral of Mallorca. He seems to have been responsible for the execution of the drawing in plate 22. See also notes 73, 77, 108.

Domingo Sugrañes Gras (died 1938) inherited the works of the Sagrada Familia. He also took part in the construction of "Bell Esguard" and the Finca Miralles. See note 77.

92. Among these younger assistants, most of whom have published extensively their recollections of Gaudí, should be listed:

The present architects of the Sagrada Familia: Luis Bonet y Garí (1893—), Isidro Puig Boada (1891—), Francisco de Paula Quintana (1892—). The architects Juan Bergós Massó (1894—), Francisco Folguera Grassi (1891—), César Martinell Brunet (1888—), José F. Ráfols (1889—). The sculptor Juan Matamala Flotats (1893—). The painter Ricardo Opisso Sala (1880—), who was a friend of Picasso in their youth.

See the bibliography for their publications.

93. The critic Feliu Elías ("Joan Sacs") had published exaggerated reports which he had received of Berenguer's contribution. Gaudí's associates corrected him as accurately as was possible in a case where Gaudí himself had called Berenguer "my right arm." The arguments, which contain a lot of data on Gaudí's career, occurred in F. Elías *Escultura* (1928); *L'Opinió* 26 May 1928; *La Nau* 12 and 21 Dec. 1928, 2 and 9 Jan. 1929; *La Veu de Catalunya* 2, 6, 10, 19, 22, 29, and 30? March 1929, (all of Barcelona).

94. Certainly Gaudí was respected. His fellow architects wrote most enthusiastically about his buildings in Rogent *Arquitectura.* Puig y Cadafalch was full of admiration for Gaudí as a man and as an architect (interview in *El Debate* of Madrid, 13 June 1926).

95. The architect de Serra Martínez relates how he and Jerónimo Martorell, another friend of Gaudí, defended Gaudí before the Association when his membership was suspended because he had donated his "tithes" to the Sagrada Familia.

96. There does not seem to have any effort to collect these. The most slavish pastiches are not necessarily by his closest associates. See also note 63.

97. A statistical analysis of the literature that has appeared on Gaudí and his buildings should cast some light on the intensity and extent of his influence over the years.

Of the 1000-odd references to books and articles that are listed in the Gaudí archive at Columbia University, approximately one-third are dedicated to the Sagrada Familia church. However, a good portion of the latter are concerned with the cult and not with the architecture of that enterprise. Three quarters of the total literature listed was published in Catalonia, which seems natural, but the bulk of the rest appeared abroad, there being only a tiny fraction of articles about Gaudí printed elsewhere in Spain. Thus Gaudí has produced little or no stir in the rest of the peninsula, even in recent years when the literature on him has burgeoned remarkably.

In Catalonia, except during the Civil War, something has been printed every year since 1900, there having been very few articles before that date. Special numbers of periodicals dedicated to Gaudí have appeared about every five years since 1900. Throughout all of Spain the greatest interest in him seems to have been evoked during 1906–07, 1914–15, 1921–22, three apparent crises in the works of the Sagrada Familia church that were attended by publicity campaigns for funds; and during 1926–28 on the occasion of his death and memorials. Publications increased in the late 1940s and have continued steadily, with a peak in 1952, his centenary year.

Abroad, surprisingly enough, there has been a regular, if modest, output of publications and notices about Gaudí since about 1903. They fell off during the late 1930s and early 1940s, but since 1948–49 they have appeared with increasing intensity and represent the major countries that publish architectural magazines. Greatest interest has always been shown in the United States, Italy, France, Germany and Great Britain, more or less in that order, with occasional responses from Latin America and Japan. Apparently the earliest notices abroad appeared in the United States in 1892. And America, with Italy, touched off the recent interest in Gaudí: a Spanish language periodical of New York City devoted a special issue to Gaudí in 1949 with articles by Catalan experts. Alberto Sartoris and Bruno Zevi were the early enthusiasts in Italy.

As to monographs, there have been only two books on Gaudí published outside of Spain, one American (see Hitchcock) and one Italo-French (see Martinell, both very small. Books on Gaudí and the Sagrada Familia have appeared at two points—just after his death (1928–29) and since 1950 in connection with his centenary celebrations.

In an appendix to his biography of 1952, Ráfols gives a summary of the subsequent influence of Gaudí as observed in Barcelona itself; a later, international discussion of Gaudí studies is to be found in H. R. Hitchcock, "Gaudí today," *Ark* no. 17 (summer 1956), pp. 14–18.

98. Naturally the Association was not as active from July 1936 when its church was sacked. Its periodical, *El Propagador,* was suspended from July 1936 to November 1943. See also note 80.

99. J. A. Gaya Nuño's article about Gaudí's centenary in *Insula* (Madrid) 15 Sept. 1952 was reprinted in *Solidaridad Nacional* (Barcelona) 22 Oct. 1952 under the title "Grave insulto contra Gaudí." The battle raged through *Solaridad* 7 and 13 Nov. 1952; *Destino* 18 Oct. and 1 Nov. 1952; *Revista* 9 Oct. 1952—all of Barcelona; and *Indice* (Madrid) 30 Jan. 1953.

100. "De la beauté terrifiante et comestible, de l'architecture modern' style," *Minotaur,* no. 3 & 4 (1933), pp. 69–76.

101. For example, Maurice Casteels in his influential *L'art moderne primitif* (Paris: Jonquiéres, 1930) described the Casa Milá as "orné d'abcès," and commented, "Heureusement le monstre est cloué sur place...." But there were notable and enthusiastic exceptions:

Among the several comments by Le Corbusier during his visit to Barcelona in 1928 were, "This man does all that he wishes with stone.... What formidable domination of structures! ... Among the men of his generation he is the one of greatest architectonic

power..." *La Publicitat,* 18 May 1928, and *La Veu de Catalunya,* 21 May 1928.

And when Walter Gropius was interviewed in Barcelona in 1932, he stated, "Gaudí, among the architects of the old school interests me from the point of view of construction, some of the walls of the Sagrada Familia being of a marvelous technical perfection." *Hoja oficial de lunes* (Barcelona) 28 March 1932.

102. Quoted in Thomas E. Tallmadge, "The Expiatory Temple of the Holy Family," *Western Architect,* XXXI (March 1922), p. 37.

103. The main events of Gaudí's career and complete inventories of his works were published in the late 1920s, most thoroughly by Ráfols (1929), on the basis of the extensive archive in Gaudí's studio at the Sagrada Familia church. As these records and all Gaudí's drawings and plans were burned during the incidents of July 1936, we are today largely dependent on what Ráfols and others had extracted and published previously. Little serious effort has been made to check their data through other sources, and very few new projects or works have come to light since. Materials turn up from time to time in the possession of his former assistants, his patrons, etc. See note 118.

104. The question of Gaudí's birthplace is an open one, hotly contested now for several years between Reus and the adjacent town of Riudoms. Civil records of births were not kept in that area until 1870. Was he born in Reus, where his baptism was recorded on the following day, or on the family farm "Mas de la Calderera," which was situated just over the town line in Riudoms? Gaudí's own statements on the subject, oral and written, are contradictory. Documentary evidence unearthed by Guix Sugrañes of Reus would seem to favor Reus as the place of birth. For the polemic and the facts of the case, consult:

Bergós 1954, p. 13 and notes on p. 167.
J. M. Guix Sugrañes, articles in *Reus* for 26 July and 29 Nov. 1952; 1 May 1954.
Various articles in *Destino* (Barcelona) for 5 July, 2 and 30 Aug. 1952; 29 Dec. 1956; 12 Jan. and 9 Feb. 1957.

105. Although Gaudí's friend Eduardo Toda intended to leave his own series of this magazine to the municipal archive in the Casa de Arcediano of Barcelona, it cannot be located there.

106. This project, carried out with his schoolmates José Rivera (later a surgeon in Madrid) and Eduardo Toda (later a Spanish diplomat), marks an important step in Spain's Medieval Revival. Toda, a bibliofile, Maecenas, and benefactor of the Biblioteca Central of Barcelona, continued his interest in the monastery and seems to have been a prime mover in its eventual restoration. The school project, a manuscript of some sixty pages in eight chapters, has apparently disappeared, but it was described in detail by J. Barrera in *El Correo Catalán,* 1 to 6 Oct. 1926. Toda published a short, un-illustrated version in 1870: *Poblet: descripción histórica* (Reus: Torquelles y Zamora). See note 6.

107. This is the dating of Bergós, which takes into account several years of preparation on Gaudí's part after he arrived in Barcelona (Bergós 1954, p. 16 and notes).

107a. The Municipal Museum of Reus possesses a

sheet on which Gaudí jotted down historical data and sketches for a student problem, that of a Spanish pavilion at the Philadelphia Centennial Exposition. He had planned to decorate the stand with names from Catalan history that had been associated with Roger de Flor's expedition to Philadelphia of Asia Minor in the year 1304. The museum also has two handwritten treatises on the siting and construction of churches and on the virtues of country houses that probably formed part of his writings of 1876–78.

108. The decision to finish the facade of their cathedral in the Castilian rather than Catalan or even Victorian Gothic style appears to have been a turning point in the local Medieval Revival. Augusto Font's design was accepted and executed (1882–1912) despite preference by the press and by influential artistic organizations for that of Juan Martorell. Martorell published pamphlets in defense of his project in 1882 and 1883, and was vigorously seconded by his followers Gaudí and Doménech y Montaner. Gaudí's rendering was used in the campaign (figure 25). See Juan Rubió y Bellver, *Tàber Mons Barcinonensis* (Barcelona: Casa P. de Caritat, 1927), pp. 23 ff.

109. There is some confusion as to the date that Gaudí began work on this building. Del Villar relinquished the project in 1883. Puig Boada and others, who had access to records now lost, state that Gaudí accepted the commission on 3 Nov. 1883 (Puig Boada, *S.F.*, 1929, p. 11). Probably construction was not resumed until 1884. *El Propagador,* official organ of the enterprise, made no mention of the change at the time and gave contradictory dates in later accounts.

110. This building has usually been dated 1892–94. However, Gaudí was apparently first approached in 1890, and his plans are dated December 1891. The structure then took two years to build. The history of the firm and of the building is related in articles in *Destino* (Barcelona), 18 April and 9 May, 1953, and in *León,* a local magazine, for May 1954.

The idea of placing St. George, the patron saint of Catalonia, on a Leonese building was resented locally. But when, because of "deterioration," it was removed in the 1950's, *La Vanguardia Española* of Barcelona led a campaign for its replacement, which was carried out in 1956 (*Vanguardia,* 21 Dec. 1952, 4 Feb. 1953, 10 July 1956; *Destino,* 27 Dec. 1952).

111. One rose window and two lancets were designed by Gaudí and in part carried out by assistants. The windows were made of four laminations of glass: yellow, blue, red, and white, the unwanted hues removed from the design by acid. This system of Gaudí was calculated to produce unusual brilliance of light and an infinite range of colors. (See Puig Boada, *S.F.,* 1952, p. 125).

112. Ráfols had dated the pulpits 1912, but later research at Blanes points to this earlier date. See José M. Garrut, "Una obra poco conocida de Antonio Gaudí," in *Templo* XC (Feb. 1955), p. 6.

113. For this planning see Ráfols 1929, pp. 115 ff; Bergós 1954, pp. 152–53; *Calendario* 1927, p. 22; *El Propagador,* 1 April 1927; and *La Noche* (Barcelona), 7 April 1927.

114. Other exhibitions of Gaudí's work during his lifetime were held in Madrid 1911, Gerona 1915, Olot 1915, Reus 1916, crypt of the Sagrada Familia 1917, Valls 1917, and as part of a general exposition of liturgical art in Barcelona 1925.

115. Gaudí was also featured in the second Exposition of Liturgical Art in 1928. This appears to have been the last exhibition of his work until the centenary of his birth in the 1950s—photographs of his works being included in the Spanish exhibit at the Milan Triennial of 1951.

116. For "The Strange Architecture of Antonio Gaudí," in *The Listener.*

117. This shrine was to be similar to that of the Madre de Dios planned for the north cloister of the Sagrada Familia church and described in *Album Record a Gaudí* (Barcelona, 1936), pp. 91–93. The request from Chile was reported in *Calendario* 1927, p. 23. Gaudí's correspondence with Chile on the matter is lost. Bishop Larraín of Rancagua has reported, through Malte Crasemann of Santiago, that no information can be found in their archive there.

118. To complete this inventory, it should be mentioned that the architect Bonet y Garí owns a drawing by Gaudí for a monument to Prat de la Riba (1918); the architect Quintana has drawings for lamps; the sculptor Juan Matamala has a photograph of a workshop constructed by Gaudí for one of his assistants. The Amigos de Gaudí of Barcelona are attempting to collect and preserve such fragments.

FIGURE 25.

SELECTED BIBLIOGRAPHY

WHERE appropriate, a comment is included after the listing to explain the value of the item.

To save space most books and articles on special subjects which are cited in the Notes are not repeated here, but may be located through their subject entry in the Index (pp. 135–136). However, titles that are used throughout the text in abbreviated form will be found listed here in full.

Almost without exception the items cited in this book can be consulted in the archive of the Amigos de Gaudí U.S.A. (in the Department of Fine Arts and Archaeology of Columbia University) or in neighboring libraries.

A large part of this material, including much that is basic, is written in Catalan.

(A) Basic books or pamphlets dedicated to Gaudí. These include monographs, picture books and anthologies of articles, but not publications dedicated to single buildings, which can be located in the Notes by consulting the Index.

[various]. *Antoni Gaudí: La seva vida, les seves obres, la seva mort* (Barcelona: Políglota, 1926). See note 19.

Juan Bergós, *Gaudí: l'home i l'obra* (Barcelona: Ariel, 1954). Invaluable and up-to-date. 184 illustrations.

Juan Eduardo Cirlot, *El Arte de Gaudí* (Barcelona: Omega, 1st ed. 1950, 2nd ed. 1954).

Henry-Russell Hitchcock, *Gaudí* (New York: Museum of Modern Art [1957]). Illustrated catalog of the Museum's exhibition.

Le Corbusier, J. Gomis and J. Prats Vallés, *Gaudí: fotoscop* (Barcelona: RM, 1958). 61 dramatic photographs.

Arturo Llopis, *Gaudí en la Villa de Gracia* (Barcelona: Arolas, n.d.). Obscure but useful pamphlet of recollections.

César Martinell, *Antonio Gaudí* (Milano: Electa, 1955). Well-illustrated booklet in Astra-Arengarium series.

idem., Gaudinismo (Barcelona: Amigos de Gaudí, 1954). A compilation of the author's writings on Gaudí.

Francesc Pujols, *La visió artística i religiosa d'En Gaudí* (Barcelona: Catalonia, 1927). Rare and fascinating essay by a Catalan critic.

José F. Ráfols and Francisco Folguera, *Gaudí, el gran arquitecto español* (Barcelona: Canosa, 1st ed. in Catalan 1928, 2nd ed. in Spanish 1929). See note 103. This, the basic tool for Gaudí studies, contains a chronology, twenty pages of bibliography and about 275 illustrations that show many works now lost.

J. F. Ráfols, *Gaudí: 1852–1926* (Barcelona: Aedos, 1952). A rather more discursive volume with less data and illustrations, but additional bibliography.

(B) Periodicals and newspapers have frequently dedicated special numbers or supplements to the works of Gaudí. Among the more important are:

Calendario 1927. See under "D" below. Basic biographical details.

Catalunya Social, Barcelona, VI (19 June 1926). Literary essays.

Chiesa e quartiere, Bologna, no. 5 (March 1958). Useful.

La ciutat i la casa, Barcelona, III, no. 6 (1927).

La Cronica de Valls, Valls in Catalonia (7 April 1917). Sagr. Familia.

Cuadernos de arquitectura, Barcelona, no. 26 (1956). Pictorially exciting, new plans, old caricatures.

Cupula, Barcelona, no. 319 (1952?). 11 informative articles.

De l'art de la forja, Barcelona, I (March 1921). Gaudí's ironwork.

Forma, Barcelona, II, no. 16 (1907). Essays by J. Pijoan and J. Maragall.

Gaseta de les arts, Barcelona, III (1 July 1926). Unique photographs of Gaudí's studio.

La Hormiga de Oro, Barcelona, XLIV (17 March 1923). Sagr. Familia.

Ilustració Catalana (18 March 1906), Sagr. Familia; and (19 June 1910).

El Matí, Barcelona (21 June 1936). A newspaper supplement containing more than 25 articles on Gaudí, many of them basic.

Papeles de Son Armadans, Madrid and Palma, IV (Dec. 1959).

El Propagador (see under "D" below) dedicated special numbers to Gaudí or the Sagr. Familia on the following occasions: XLIX (15 May 1915) Sagr. Familia; LX (1 & 15 July 1926) see note 19; LX (1 & 15 Aug. 1926) illustrated chronology of Sagr. Familia works; LXI (1 June 1927) memorial lectures (see Chronol. 1926, p. 32); LXII (1 June 1928); LXVI (1932), pp. 80 ff., more illustrated history of Sagr. Familia works.

Proyectos y Materiales, New York, V (Sept.–Oct. 1949), see note 97.

Revista (Barcelona) 31 May & 6 June 1956. Useful articles on occasion of the Gaudí exhibition.

Revista Nacional de Arquitectura, Madrid XIII (July 1953). Report of a symposium on Gaudí.

Revista Nova, Barcelona, I (23 May 1914).

Templo (see under "D" below) dedicated special numbers to Gaudí or the Sagrada Familia on the following occasions: LXXXVI (June 1951); LXXXVII (April–May 1952) Sagr. Familia; LXXXVII (Aug. 1952); XCI (April 1956) Sagr. Familia; XCIII (Sept. 1958).

(C) The following is a list of articles on Gaudí that have an interest for their critical point of view, for their factual content, or for their availability in languages other than Spanish. It is a small fraction of the articles that have appeared on him and does not ordinarily include those in the special issues listed in "B" or articles on special subjects cited in the Notes.

Dore Ashton, "Antonio Gaudí," *Craft Horizons,* New York, XVII (Nov.–Dec. 1957).

E. and R. Burckhardt, "The Unfinished Cathedral and Antonio Gaudí," *Art News* LVI (Jan. 1958).

Antonio Cassi Ramelli, "Mestiere e maestria di Antonio Gaudí," *Archittetura: cantiere,* Milan, no. 11 (Dec. 1956).

Ramiro de Maeztu, "El arquitecto del naturalismo," *Nuevo Mundo* (Madrid), 16 March, 1911.

F. L. P. Dewald, "Antonio Gaudí, spaans architect," *Bouwkundig weekblad,* Amsterdam, LXXV (19 March 1957).

César Ferrater, "Gaudí en el Museo Municipal de Reus," *Reus* (28 June 1952). Little-known works illustrated.

P. L. F[louquet], "Surréalisme et architecture: a propos de Gaudí y Cornet," *La Maison,* Brussels, VIII (Nov. 1952).

C. Giedion-Welcker, "Bildhafte Kachel-Kompositen von Antonio Gaudí," *Werk,* Zurich, XLII (April 1955).

H. R. Hitchcock, "The work of Antoni Gaudí i Cornet," *Architectural Association Journal,* London, LXXIV (Nov. 1958).

Oswaldo Jimeno, "Antonio Gaudí y la originalidad arquitectonica," *El arquitecto peruano,* Lima (July–Aug. 1953).

Anthony Kerrigan, "Gaudianism in Catalonia," *Arts,* New York, XXXII (Dec. 1957).

Marius-Ary Leblond, "Gaudí el l'architecture méditerranéenne," *L'art et les artistes,* Paris, XI (1910), pp. 69 ff. An influential early critique.

Paul Linder, "Encuentros con Antoni Gaudí," *Mar del Sur,* Lima, II (Mar.–Apr. 1950). Interesting reminiscences.

Alberto Moravia, "Gaudí," *Corriere della sera* (Milan), 6 May 1954.

Ricardo Opisso, a series of informative recollections in *Diario de Barcelona,* 24 Nov. 1950; 24 March, 5 July, 30 Aug., & 2 Dec., 1951; 25 June, 20 July 1952; 21 Jan. and 22 March 1953; 3 Oct. 1956.

Bengt Pettersson, "Antonio Gaudí ett ornamentikens geni," *Sydsvenska Dagbladet,* Malmö, 27 Feb. 1955.

Nikolaus Pevsner, "The Strange Architecture of Antonio Gaudí," *The Listener,* London, XLVIII (7 Aug. 1952). See Chronol. 1952–53, p. 32.

Francisco de P. Quintana, "Conferencia. . .," *Templo,* LXXXVII (Aug. 1952). Very comprehensive discussion of Gaudí.

[Carlo L. Ragghianti], "Antoni Gaudí," *Sele arte,* Ivrea, VI (Mar.–Apr. 1958).

Amós Salvador, "Un recuerdo de Gaudí," *Arquitectura,* Madrid, IX, no. 93 (1927).

Alberto Sartoris, "Gaudí poliforme," *Numero,* Florence, no. 3 (Dec. 1952).

Robert Schoelkopf, "Antonio Gaudí, architect," *Perspecta,* New Haven, no. 2, [1953].

José Luis Sert, "Introduzione a Gaudí," *Casabella,* Milan, no. 202 (Aug.–Sept. 1954). A chapter of his forthcoming book.

Idem, "Gaudí, visionnaire et précurseur," *L'Oeil,* Paris, no. 2 (15 Feb. 1955).

Poul E. Skriver, "Gaudí," *Arkitekten,* Copenhagen, no. 18 (Sept. 1959).

J. M. Sostres Maluquer, "Sentimiento y simbolismo del espacio," *Proyectos y Materiales,* New York, V (Sept.–Oct. 1949).

Idem, "El funcionalismo y la nueva plástica," *Boletín de información de la Dirección general de Arquitectura,* Madrid, IV (July 1950).

Domingo Sugrañes, "Gaudí i l'urbanisme," *El Matí* (Barcelona), 31 July 1932.

J. J. Sweeney, "Antoni Gaudí," *Magazine of Art,* New York, XLVI (May 1953).

Idem, "Is yesterday's fantasy tomorrow's working geometry?" *Arch. Forum,* New York, CIV (March 1956).

Umberto Tavanti, "Un architecto independente: Antonio Gaudí," *Vita d'Arte,* Siena, V (1910), pp. 25 ff.

Nils Tesch, "Antonio Gaudí," *Byggmästaren,* Stockholm, no. 10 (1948). First long non-Spanish article on Gaudí since the early 1930s.

Evelyn Waugh, "Gaudí," *Arch. Review,* London, LXVII (June 1930). "Discovery" of Gaudí. Reprinted in *Labels* (London: Duckworth, 1930) pp. 172–82.

Bruno Zevi, "Un genio catalano: Antonio Gaudí," *Metron,* Rome, no. 38 (Sept.–Oct. 1950). A landmark in post-war rediscovery of Gaudí.

(D) The only one of Gaudí's works about which a full length monograph has appeared is the Church of the Sagrada Familia. The following is a portion of the immense bibliography on it:

The bookstore, Librería Herederos de la Vda. Pla (see note 36) has from time to time published small booklets and large albums with photographs and essays about the Sagrada Familia, for sale at the site. The title varies; editions have been printed in 1915, c. 1917, 1925, 1936, 1947, 1952.

The bookstore also published a periodical, *El Propagador de la Devoción a San José* (1867–1936, 1943–48) which has been continued as *Templo* since 1948. From 1915–36 an annual *Calendario Josefina* was issued at year-end for the following year. All are full of articles on Gaudí and the church works—see listings in Ráfols 1929 and 1952.

BOOKS:

A. Cirici Pellicer, J. Gomis, J. Prats Vallés, *La Sagrada Familia: fotoscop* (Barcelona: Omega, 1952). 80 striking pictures.

César Martinell, *Gaudí i la Sagrada Familia comentada per ell mateix* (Barcelona: Aymá, 1951). Anthology of Gaudí's ideas on architecture—see note 82.

Idem, La Sagrada Familia (Barcelona: Aymá, 1952).

Isidro Puig Boada, *El Temple de la Sagrada Familia* (Barcelona: Barcino, 1929). This first edition of the standard book on the building is in Catalan. It has been republished in Spanish with many more plates (Barcelona: Omega, 1952).

ARTICLES:

Discussions of the building have appeared in *L'Osservatore Romano* on 18 Dec. 1921, 6 Jan. 1922, 3 Oct. 1952.

Special items in *El Propagador* and *Templo* that should be mentioned are a report on the war destruction in the former (LXXVIII, 1943, pp. 4–8); in the latter a history of the models (LXXXIII, Feb. 1948), and a chronicle of the enterprise (LXXXV, Oct. 17, 1951).

An interesting report from Madrid is in *El Universo,* 7 & 8 Dec. 1914.

Mildred Stapley, "The story of the creation told in stone in the great new cathedral of Barcelona," *The Craftsman,* New York, XXI, no. 5 (1912).

Anton Henze, "Antonio Gaudís Sühnetempel der heiligen Familie," in *Festschrift Martin Wackernagel* (Cologne: Böhlau, 1958).

Kenji Imai, "Architecture of Barcelona: Sagrada Familia Cathedral," *Kentiku Sekai,* Tokyo, no. 8 (Aug. 1939).

A. Lambert, "Die Kirche Sagrada Familia in Barcelona," *Deutsche Bauzeitung,* Berlin, LX (15 May 1926).

Juan Maragall published essays on the building in *Diario de Barcelona,* 19 Dec. 1900, 7 Nov. 1905, 19 March 1906, and in *Ilustració Catalana,* 15 Jan. 1905. They can be found in his collected works. See notes 5, 14.

Fritz Mielert, "Vom modernen Kirchenbau in Spanien," *Archiv f. Christl. Kunst,* Stuttgart, XXVIII (1910), pp. 76 ff.

P. M. Stratton, "The Sagrada Familia Church," *The Builder,* London, CXXXIII (5 Aug. 1927).

L. Z[ahn], "Antonio Gaudí und seine Kathedrale" *Das Kunstwerk,* Baden-Baden, IX, heft 5 (1955–56).

(E) Gaudí is discussed in many general books on art, architecture and Spain. His works are invariably mentioned in travel books, guide books, biographical dictionaries, picture books of Catalonia and in general surveys of Spanish art. These are too numerous to list here, but we cite a few that are of interest and have not appeared in the Notes:

Louis Bréhier, *L'art chrétien* (Paris: Laurens, 1918), pp. 415–16.

Francisco Gras y Elías, *Hijos ilustres de Reus* (Barcelona: Puig y Alfonso, 1899), p. 97.

H. R. Hitchcock, *Architecture: 19th and 20th Centuries* (Baltimore: Penguin, 1958), *passim*.

Kenji Imai, *Modern Architecture in Europe* (Tokyo: Waseda Univ., 1928), II.

Nikolaus Pevsner, *Wegbereiter moderner Formgebung* (Hamburg: Rowohlt, 1957), p. 8.

Alberto Sartoris, *Encyclopédie de l'architecture nouvelle* (Milan: Hoepli, 1948–54), I, p. 110 Post-war "rediscovery"; edition of 1957 contains more.

Bruno Zevi, *Storia dell'architettura moderna* (Torino: Einaudi, 1950) pp. 87–88 and *passim*.

(F) BACKGROUND: books, periodicals and articles that discuss or illustrate aspects of Catalan art and architecture between about 1850 and 1950. Most of these take up Gaudí as part of the general ambient. Monographs or articles dealing with specific architects among his forerunners, contemporaries, assistants and followers are listed in the Notes and can be located by consulting the individual's name in the Index.

Album artístich de la Renaixensa (Barcelona, 1882–88). Collection of plates that were issued by subscription.

Album d'architecture moderne à Barcelona (Barcelona: Parera, 1911), similar.

The former Asociación de arquitectos de Cataluña published three serials that are full of illustrative material and valuable articles:
  Revista (1893–97);
  Arquitectura y construcción (1897–1923?);
  Anuario (1899–1929, some years being combined), cumulative index to *Anuario* in *Cuadernos de Arquitectura* IV (May 1947).

Oriol Bohigas, "La arquitectura catalana moderna en seis fechas," *Revista* (Barcelona), 3–9 May 1956.

A. Cirici Pellicer, *Picasso antes de Picasso* (Barcelona: Iberia, 1946).

G. Desdevises du Dezert, "L'art catalan moderne," *Revue des Pyrénées,* Toulouse, XV (1903), pp. 1–10.

Idem, Barcelone et les grands sanctuaires catalans (Paris: Laurens, 1913).

Documentos de Arte y Decoración (Barcelona: Parera, n.d.). Similar to the Albums above.

Feliu Elías ("Joan Sacs"), *L'Escultura Catalana moderna* (Barcelona: Barcina, 1928), 2 vols.

P. M. F[itzgerald] & D. F., "The Arts in Modern Spain," *World Review,* London, n.s. XXII (Dec. 1950). Good report.

Enric Jardí, "Renaissance catalane: architecture," in *L'Art Public,* Brussels, (Dec. 1909).

"Katalanische Impressionen," *National Zeitung* (Basle) 26 Jan. 1953.

César Martinell, *L'art català sota la unitat espanyola* (Barcelona: Canosa, 1933).

Idem, "Veinticinco años de arquitectura barcelonsa: 1908–33," *Barcelona Atracción* (May 1933).

Victor Ottmann, "Die phantastische Stadt," *Die Woche* (Berlin) 28 Aug. 1926.

J. F. Ráfols, *El arte romántico en España* (Barcelona: Juventud, 1954).

Idem, Diccionario biográfico de artistas de Cataluña (Barcelona: Millá, 1951–54) 3 vols. Indispensable!

F. Rogent y Pedrosa and L. Doménech y Montaner, et al., *Arquitectura moderna de Barcelona* (Barcelona: Perera, 1897–1900?). Issued similarly to the Albums above.

Maria Rusiñol, *Santiago Rusiñol vist per la seva filla* (Barcelona: Aedos, 1950).

Emmanuel Sorra, "L'architecture catalane contemporaine," *L'art decoratif,* Paris, I (1908), pp. 201–18.

Carlos Soldevila, *Cataluña: sus hombres y sus obras* (Barcelona: Aedos, 1955). Many thumb-nail sketches of the intellectual figures of Gaudí's day. Illustrated.

Wolfgang Weber, *Barcelona* (Berlin: Albertus, 1928). Good photographs.

(G) BACKGROUND: The following deal more specifically with aspects of Modernismo, the Spanish Art Nouveau, usually treating Gaudí as well:

The movement and the subsequent classicistic reaction to it can be followed in two different series of local *avant-garde* periodicals: *Luz* (1898), *Quatre Gats* (1899), *Pel & Ploma* (1899–1903), *Forma* (1904–08); *Joventut* (1900–1906), *Garba* (1906—).

R. Benet and R. Llates, *Quatre Gats* (Barcelona: Barna, 1954). Catalog of the exhibit of Modernista painting at the Sala Parés.

A. Cirici Pellicer, *El arte modernista catalán* (Barcelona: Aymá, 1951). With its more than 500 illustrations, color plates and facsimiles and its masses of biographical data, this volume is basic for study of the period.

La Esquella de la Torratxa XX (17 June 1898). Contemporary issue of one of Barcelona's leading humor magazines devoted to a caricature of Modernismo.

James Grady, "A Bibliography of the Art Nouveau," *J. of the Society of Architectural Historians* XIV (May 1955). See also note 54.

Stephen Tschudi Madsen, *Sources of Art Nouveau* (New York: Wittenborn, 1955).

J. F. Ráfols, *Modernismo y modernistas* (Barcelona: Destino, 1949). Somewhat more literary and anecdotal in character, this is a valuable complement to Cirici's volume for Catalan studies. It is an expansion of Ráfols' smaller book, *El arte modernista en Barcelona* (Barcelona: Dalmau, 1943).

Idem, "Valoración de Gaudí por los de *Pel & Ploma,*" *Destino* (Barcelona) 14 Dec. 1957.

INDEX